I0456506

God is Always Chasing After You
with
Smiles to Share

A collection to encourage connection with one another for those experiencing a healing journey of critical illness or loss.

Kelly May Harris

Illustrated by Dave O'Connell

The LORD will guide you always; he will satisfy your needs in a sun-scorched land and will strengthen your frame. You will be like a well-watered garden, like a spring whose waters never fail.

Isaiah 58:11

Name: Harris, Kelly May
Title: *God Is Always Chasing After You* by Kelly May Harris
Illustrations: Dave O'Connell
Interior and cover layouts: Robert Ousnamer

ISBN: 978-1-955309-72-1
LCCN: 2023918952
Subjects: 1. Family &Relationships/ Death, Grief, Bereavement
2. Books > Family & Relationships/ Activities
3. Books > Religion/ Christian Living/ Death, Grief, Bereavement

Published by EABooks Publishing
a division of Living Parables of Central Florida, Inc.
eabookspublishing.com

I write this book in honor of my daughter Kayla Elizabeth Harris.

Child,
    Your desire to "help others smile," continues to shine a light for Jesus into the world. We hurt big my Darling, but God is love, and Love is getting us through.

Love always,
Momma

Table of Contents

God Is Always Chasing After You

Introduction:
Faith vs. Feelings

Dear Reader,

An incident occurred early in my life that made death and dying—or the fear of it—run my life. Subsequently, I felt terrified and hunted by anything and everything.

One afternoon Great Grandpa and I were preparing for his nap after spending the morning together. Like normal, he sat on the bed, and I headed to the kitchen for his cup of warm milk, bread, and honey prepared by Grandma or Mom. I'd always come back to the bedroom to find him "sleeping." His fake sleep would end as I walked away, and he would startle me by sitting up. "Got you!" he'd cry as I'd jump in alarm.

I'm going to get him this time! I, six, thought as I set his cup down and turned to tiptoe away.

Trying not to giggle, I turned back quickly. "Got you!" I blurted.

This time Great Grandpa didn't sit up; he didn't "get" me. I noticed his tummy area wasn't moving, but I didn't say a word.

A while later, when we left Great Grandpa's house, I was buckled up in the back of the tan station wagon and knew if I talked to Mom while she drove, she wouldn't be able to hear me well over the noise from the muffler and open windows. But I couldn't keep it in any longer. "Momma, Great Grandpa's tummy wasn't moving," I said.

Mom paused. "Are you sure?" I nodded. What came after that is a blur as Mom, and soon everyone else, learned Great Grandpa had died. That was the day I learned silence could be deafening.

Death became something I feared, and sleep became a second priority to watching over others. Every. Single. Night.

When I thought all were asleep, as a six-year-old child, I'd peer into every room to watch for tummies to move. As I realized my

1

loved ones were breathing, then, and only then, would I let myself rest.

This fear and night watch continued well into my adult years. When I came to learn the One True God, the Alpha and Omega, loved us enough to have a plan and sent His Son to remove the sting of death, this urge lessened. Over time, with the help of the Holy Spirit, my faith grew, and I learned to hold onto hope through life-threatening illnesses and deaths of loved ones. I learned to feel a confidence that healing would come, either in this life or the next. The question that existed was: In which realm would the healing occur? In the physical world—the one we see, touch, hear, feel, taste—or the spiritual realm, the unseen eternal existence.

Praise be to God! I no longer feared death. At least I didn't until my daughter Kayla became critically ill with cancer. During this time and after, I experienced, and dare I say still experience, a tug-of-war between faith and feelings deeper than I'd known possible before.

Having this peace that death wasn't something to fear, while being terrified Kayla could die, felt wrong. I felt my fear was selfish. Yet, as a parent it felt, and still sometimes feels, equally wrong to have peace when a child is desperately ill.

While I struggled with these opposing feelings, I bore the responsibility to be there for everyone, especially Kayla then, and Haley, my youngest daughter, now. Self-talk, like the silence in the back of that tan station wagon, can be deafening.

If I love her, I don't want her to leave me.
You know God loves her. He has a plan for her.
If I fear her leaving, I am lacking faith.
No, if you fear her going to Heaven to be healed;
You are human.
Did I do something to bring this on?
No, *there is* No *condemnation for those who are in Christ.*
How dare you make this about yourself.
She is in pain. She is scared. Get over yourself, woman!
You are not in control. God is in control.
This is not a surprise to Him.
Stop! Be still.
Lord really? Why? I don't see how this is good.

God Is Always Chasing After You

I won't even begin to pen all the thoughts; suffice to say, this tug of war between faith and feelings is a force to be reckoned with when you are facing your own mortality, or that of someone you love. But it is okay to have this tug-of-war. If it weren't, Jesus would have told us so, and He would not have wept for Lazarus.

Scripture:

Peace I leave with you; my peace I give you.
I do not give to you as the world gives. Do not let your
hearts be troubled and do not be afraid.

John 14:27

LOVE Affirmed:

When you're secure in your tomorrow, today doesn't seem so frightening.

Once I was so frightened and lived in extreme fear, yet, I was given peace and hope. My life transformed from fear-based to freedom-based through faith in Jesus Christ. God, being love such as He is, allowed that hope, freedom, and grace to be shared with my family. This means it is okay to have happiness during our storm!

Being covered in flesh in a fallen world is our human experience. We face a constant battle to remember how big God is, which intensifies when we are hurting, when we are watching someone we love hurt, or when that person we loved has been called home for healing. We must remember to hold God and His promises through His Son Jesus closer than anything and anyone else.

Despite being unsure of where her tomorrow would be—here or in Heaven—Kayla had wisdom, peace, and praise in every part of her trials. She knew tomorrow would come; her question was simply, where would tomorrow be spent? On earth, in this Spirit-filled vessel of our sin-prone flesh and fallen world, or eternally with our Creator through our Lord and Savior Jesus Christ. She had no need to fear the last.

Perhaps you are struggling in a tug of war of feelings and faith with your own critical illness, with the illness or death of someone you love, or perhaps you desire to gain some perspective of those

3

who are facing these issues. Perhaps this, or some other circumstance has your faith, has you, feeling fluttery, like mine felt—and still feels—at times.

The Holy Spirit led me to write this book. First and foremost, my goal is to honor and glorify God, through bits and pieces of my family's testimony through critical illness and loss.

Second, I believe He has a purpose for this sharing—perhaps to help you rest assured you're not alone in this back-and-forth dynamic between faith and feelings. **Perhaps these family stories will give you a talking tool to open up conversation and bring about connection with one another.**

And last, but not least, I write this in memory of my daughter Kayla, whose desire was to help others smile.

Each of the thirteen chapters are broken into two main sections:

Dear Reader:

The Dear Reader section is written with adults in mind; however, some teens and preteens might enjoy or benefit from them. Dear Reader will include our experience, Scripture, LOVE Affirmed, and prayer subsections.

The Scripture section is listed to help you connect with the Lord and as a means to help you fellowship with loved ones. Unless otherwise noted, all verses are from New International Version (NIV). The Goal of LOVE Affirmed is to apply Scripture to the experience and offer encouragement through it.

Prayer is simply that—a prayer over each reader. I pray this collection shares a connection, and a reassurance that, no matter the circumstance, hope exists. Not only is God with you, but so are others who have walked with God through similar experiences.

Smiles to Share:

This section is written with all audiences in mind, including families with children. For our family, one child was at the hospital with me. Her sister and cousin, who's more like a sister, were back home with loved ones. Several other family members and friends—children and adults alike who were dearly concerned for Kayla—could not visit her because of her compromised immune system.

Short of the illness and other hospital business, finding conversation points became difficult and left Kayla hesitant to talk, as she felt some people saw her only as her illness. Thankfully she knew she was so much more. She'd say, "Momma, I am more than this sick girl. Can we talk about something other than how I feel or how I am doing?"

Being a somewhat outside-of-the-box thinker, I'd share a story to prompt dialog between Kayla and myself. As time passed, I found the feeling Kayla had, the feeling of just being seen in regards to Kayla's illness extended to other areas as well. Haley, ten at the time, voiced a similar issue, "All people ask is how I am doing. I'd be better if we spoke about more than my sadness." Essentially Haley was saying, "I am more than the girl who lost her sister." That expression rings true.

My babies were so right. Kayla was and still is more than her illness. Haley was and still is more than a grieving sister. You are a chosen child of God, unique in so many ways. I see you. God sees you. To help with this on both sides of the issue our family found other things to talk about and share. This is where these Smiles to Share stories come in to play, simply as something else to talk about. Please note there is a second book titled *Smiles to Share because God's Always Chasing After You* that is available. It is a collection of the stories by themselves and includes more illustrations as well as a seek and find activity.

I pray the Smiles to Share section offers connection tools, things to discuss, and perhaps a smile or two along the way. At the end of each Smiles to Share story will be Connecting Ideas. These include big or small questions and activities that can help a family remain connected through their journey. Each has a Scripture that relates to the story. Questions were designed with children in mind, but they can serve as conversation starters for all audiences. You may be surprised at how much a conversation opens up with out-of-the ordinary questions.

Remember readers, *God is Always Chasing After You with Smiles to Share*!

Prayer:

Lord, You are the Author of our lives, and Father, You have purposed every life. Thank You for the opportunity to share our hearts. Thank You for the person reading this. You have chosen this time, this place, this circumstance—either by your active will or through Your passive will—in his or her life. I pray the words shared through these pages will be heard if it is Your desire Father that they be heard. Affirming and reassuring, yet raw and real, may these words, these stories, these experiences open and connect hearts. May whatever comes from this sharing glorify You, through the name of your Son, Jesus. May each reader know You are with him or her, and he or she needs only to seek You in the moments, even in the circumstances that surround that person. Thank you; You are faithful, Father.

Smiles to Share - Introduction

Tug-of-War

Bella Bird, my beauty, and I worked hard building our nest
when Ian and Rose came along and caused a bit of stress.
It was a tug-of-war with toys, even when there were two.
I felt bad for their dad and wondered what he would do.
He removed what they fought over and placed it in timeout
when he did this, he was calm; he did not get angry or shout.
He spoke stern yet soft, "You are in a tug-of-war I see,
I will need you to give what disturbed your peace to me."

These little humans seemed to be twins about five years old
I watched closely as the boy named Ian was pretty bold.
We chose a tree branch protected from the strong winds that blew,
close to the bottom so our chicks could be shaded, too.
Just as we thought we'd finished, ornery Ian came along,
he made us question if where we placed our nest was wrong.
They both climbed up the fence and reached out their featherless
    wings.
I sternly chirped at them, Rose stopped and let out a big scream.

Ian giggled instead, climbed down, and came back with a stick.
I flew, squawked, and carried on; I didn't like it one bit.
Rose didn't like it either. She grabbed the stick with a shout.
Dad came along; this time Ian was put in time out.
Then Dad whispered to me, "You're in a kind-of-war I see,
I'll need you Sir, to trust what disturbed your peace with me."
He removed the stick and redirected where they could play.

God Is Always Chasing After You

Bella Bird and I sang with joy. We felt safe to stay.

Every now and then, Dad allowed the kids a closer look.
When our eggs hatched, a double family selfie took.
But sure as my tail has feathers, near every single day,
Dad had to stop a tug-of-war; this is what he'd say:
He spoke stern yet soft, "You are in a tug of war I see,
I will need you to give what disturbed your peace to me."
Years went by, my Bella and I knew just where we would go.
It was fun to watch these babes and ours learn, play, and grow.

Rose came outside one day; she seemed troubled and all but
    grown,
She talked to Father (the one in the heavenly home.)
"I'm in a kind-of-war with the feelings inside of me,
I need to give You what's disturbing my peace. Help. Please?"
Bella Bird, my beauty, and I could not tell what was wrong,
but joined together and sang, Rose a feel better song.
Right there before us, like a masterpiece God's love had made.
Their whole family joined Rose and together they prayed.

Connecting Ideas:
1) What is the best color for a bird? Can you draw or color me one?
2) What is your favorite game to play?
3) Do you like the story? What is your favorite part? Why?
4) Who can you talk to when your feelings are hurt?
5) In this story, a word we hear a lot is "peace." Peace is also in Scripture. The Bible says:

Peace I leave with you; my peace I give you. I do not give to you as the world gives. Do not let your hearts be troubled and do not be afraid.
John 14:27

6) Can you think of anything else you want to talk about or ask?

(Check out www.supposewithrose.com for free downloadable coloring pages or activities.)

One
Protect and Prepare

Dear Reader,

The experience my family and I had, which brought us to this place of sharing, is not one I'd wish on anyone. When we received the first inkling of my daughter Kayla's cancer diagnosis, we desperately wanted it to be a mistake—hoping that somehow those suspicions would be flat-out wrong. We felt vulnerable and grossly unprepared.

We, her parents, weren't the only ones who thought Kayla was an exceptional child, both in her ability to learn and her ability to put what she learned into action. Being her Momma is and forever will be one of the greatest blessings of my life.

When Kayla was a young child, perhaps three years old, she was missing me. I split my time between full-time work, home, and an active role in caring for my mother. I was also expecting another bundle, Haley, at the time. While I washed the dishes one day, a pair of the brightest blue eyes ever, tugged at my shirt tail and requested we, "Watch and be 'mazed."

As odd as it is to say, every part of our journey with Kayla shining her God-given light into this world was amazing, or surprising, in many ways—from her conception to her death and even still, as God reveals more and more of His work through her life.

Our journey with cancer, at least the fighting alongside Kayla part, may not have been long, but it felt like a freight train hit from many directions, sending every fiber of our being and every facet of our lives off the rails. Kayla spent the last 124 days of her life on Earth in the hospital with more than half of that time in the Intensive Care Unit. During her stay, we had time for talking and reminiscing.

Each of the stories in this collection were influenced by those moments between Kayla, myself, and our family during the time in the hospital or after. I believe each story has a nugget of hope from the Maker Himself. He was with us during this very painful time, just as He is standing ready to be with you in your journey. Prayerfully, this sharing can help you and your family in some way, even if it's just to know you're not alone in the emotions that accompany this season of healing.

The journey of life continues for each of us, including Kayla and my mom, Debra, who passed 101 days following Kayla's promotion to Heaven. We believe we are eternal beings. We were made in the image of the one and only God, who gifted us a path to Himself through His Son, Jesus Christ.

Scripture:

For they considered not the miracle of the loaves for their heart had hardened.
Mark 6:52 (NKJV)

Through the Lord's mercies we are not consumed, Because His compassions fail not. They are new every morning; Great is Your faithfulness. "The Lord is my portion," says my soul, "Therefore I hope in Him!"
Lamentations 3:22–24 (NKJV)

Everyone was amazed and gave praise to God. They were filled with awe and said, "We have seen remarkable things today."
Luke 5:26

This is how we know what love is:
Jesus Christ laid down his life for us. And we ought to lay down our lives for our brothers and sisters.
1 John 3:16

LOVE Affirmed:

Our human nature prompts us to protect and prepare our hearts from things seen and unseen, including pain and unknown situations. In this effort to protect ourselves, anger, hurt, and intense sadness bring many—including myself, and my husband, Dustin—a temptation to feel negatively toward our Heavenly Father. When we create a barrier around our hearts, this leads us to feel unable to approach or give praise to God, or it leaves us with a desire to push loved ones away. Essentially this protecting hardens our hearts.

We need to go against our nature and let ourselves know it is okay to have these emotions and to feel as if we are in a battle. This is where intentional actions come into play. We have the choice to call out to Him, even in moans and groans, or to turn from and refuse His hand.

You are in a battle, but you are not in it alone.

Many people say, "Take one day at a time," but in the thick of it, we found looking at a whole day was too cumbersome—especially on days when the negative feelings overshadowed everything, and all the world's statistics were grim.

Dustin recalls, "I was just trying to survive and praying we all would survive. I felt limited in my knowledge to help or fully understand the medical whirlwind. I prided myself in my ability to provide for the needs of my family. How could I provide when I did not know what to provide? I have always felt one job I have had as a husband and father was to protect my family. How do you protect from something your eyes cannot see? I felt angry, confused, and overwhelmed, to say the least."

This human nature to protect and prepare our hearts, if we aren't careful, produces a barrier and a distance within the nearest relationships. I found this to be the case for me. In efforts to protect my heart and others' hearts, I found the circle of people I shared with and the amount of things I shared shrunk. While in part, this shrinking was out of necessity, given our circumstances, some, specifically the way I connected with my Heavenly Father, was not motivated by necessity. I've come to understand, in a way, it was motivated by a lack of trust in the ability of my Heavenly Father. I was protecting my heart from the hurt that would inevitably pour out

13

when I let anyone, including God, into my hurt and fear. I felt alone yet surrounded by people, and I did not understand exactly why it was such a struggle. Hebrews 11:1 refers to faith as assurance of things hoped for and conviction of things not seen. Yet, I waited to call out to the Lord and let Him in to help me in my hurt because my fear was bigger than my trust. Often compartmentalizing and attempting to schedule when I would allow my hurt to surface.

Don't get me wrong; we fervently cried out to the Lord, literally with bloodied knees, not only for the obvious pain of others around us and for Kayla and hospital personnel. But I was failing to allow God in to help me. My faith was not bigger than my fear, and I doubted God's ability to help me back up if I let myself fall. Amid intense emotions, I learned connecting with one another and our Heavenly Father is a choice we decide to make moment-by-moment, heartbeat-by-heartbeat, and breath-by-breath. Yet we must connect; it is part of God's design for our lives.

Just like the little three-year-old girl in my kitchen all those years ago who just wanted to, "watch and be 'mazed," God designed us for this connection. To maintain connection is to have victory in the battle. To maintain connection is indeed to watch and be amazed at what God can and will do in your life even when it hurts.

Prayer:
Our family witnessed some of the saddest and most beautiful parts of living as followers of Jesus Christ simultaneously, Father. Help readers strike a balance. Help each of us in the moments, heartbeats, and breaths find an uninhibited connection with You that they and others may, "watch and be 'mazed," in Your presence.

Lord, You purposed this sharing of hope and healing for families dealing with life-threatening illness, no matter whether they are new to the journey of critical illness, have lost one they love, or are seeking perspective for or from those who have been on that journey. I ask You to bring peace and comfort in such a way that only You, the I Am, the One deemed Love and Wonderful Counselor can in the lives of each reader.

Smiles to Share – Section 1

"Watch and Be Amazed"

"Watch and be 'mazed," the precious child said;
After waking briskly and jumping out of bed.
"Amazed in what?" Mom busily did say.
"I do not know yet, Momma. It's a brand new day!"

"Of course," Mom said, taken back to the day,
when whimsical wonder was her worldly display.
"Want to color, read books, or play some games?"
Mom asked her child, while placing dishes to drain.

"No," she said proudly, with her gap-toothed grin,
mentioning things she wanted to do again.
This was the meaning behind what was heard;
though not in as many or exactly these words.

"Let's explore new places; far, vast, and wide.
Let's go outside, you're the seeker, I will hide.
Let's taste falling rain, smell a bright red rose,
Feel the sand under our feet and between our toes.

Let's hear birds and listen for crickets to sing,
throw rocks in the water to watch circling rings."
The sunset drew the day quickly to close.
They ate then bathed between ten twinkling toes.

God Is Always Chasing After You

The child mumbled; her bright eyes filled with sleep.
Her blanket wrapped around her; her arms round Mommy.
"Dear God, thank you for this day. Amen.
I wish Momma could watch and be 'mazed again."

Mom prayed over her child; broke to silent tears.
Wishing days didn't so quickly turn into years.
So goes the saying, "From the mouths of babes,"
Thank you God for moments to, "watch and be amazed."

The Bible says our troubles are enough for each day.
God loves us and is with us, every step of the way.
So, friends, I pray hearts open to the wonders of His love.
And minds focus on those good things from above.

Connecting Ideas:

1)   What is amazing to you? Can you draw it?

2)   What is something you stepped in or on that made your feet messy?

3)   Do you like the story? What is your favorite part? Why?

4)   Is there someone (anyone) you want to spend a day being amazed with? What would that look like?

5)   Sometimes, we can to choose to stop what we are doing for someone else, to help that one feel loved. The Bible says:

This is how we know what love is: Jesus Christ laid down his life for us. And we ought to lay down our lives for our brothers and sisters.
1 John 3:16

6)   Can you think of anything else you want to talk about or ask?

(Check out www.supposewithrose.com for free downloadable coloring pages or activities.)

God Is Always Chasing After You

Two
Golden Game

Dear Reader,

From my perspective, integrity matters. The quality of being honest and having strong moral principles is by far one of the most important characteristics a person can have, in my opinion. This expectation of myself and of others is likely a huge source of my hurts and self-scrutiny. This characteristic rubbed off on my children as well.

When we were in the hospital, this proved to be a source of major struggle for my child who was a very literal thinker. We had nurses, doctors, resident doctors, child-life specialists, respiratory therapists, occupational therapists, music therapists, physical therapy, wound care specialists, transplant team, ICU team, nutritionist, teachers, surgeons, and medical assistants. In short, lots of people were involved in Kayla's struggle over a relatively short period of time. All of them handled various situations differently. And often, different ones had multiple opinions or approaches on the same situations. Add the fact that hospital schedules for surgeries, imaging, and doctor consultations are more fluid than water, and this resulted in a very upset Kayla! She had not quite gotten to the point of understanding that sometimes people are unable to keep their word and situations change. She held herself to this standard too.

A dainty little girl had become Kayla's neighbor at the hospital. We will call her Zoe. She and her family were also new to the cancer journey. Zoe could not have been more than three years old, and the nurses struggled to get her to move. Zoe took a great interest in Kayla's stuffed mascot BB the hen, nested on Kayla's IV pole.

Kayla saw this struggle and interest. So the next day, Kayla painted chicks on rocks and promised she would play a game with Zoe. Kayla asked Zoe if she would help BB find her chicks the next day. She explained she would go on her walk in the hall early in the morning and hide the chicks. Then, when Zoe went on her walk, she could find them and put them next to Kayla's room door. Being so very young, when Kayla showed Zoe the chicks she would be looking for, Zoe, with all her cuteness and a big smile, said, "I found them." She was happy as she could be.

The next morning proved to be a chemo side-effect day for Kayla. She did not feel up to walking outside of the room. When she heard that Zoe and her family were leaving, actually moving out of state, Kayla was troubled. She felt she'd not kept her word to hide BB's chicks. "Mom, can you please go see if I can hide them for her to play before she goes?" she asked. "I don't want her to think I didn't mean what I said."

It turned out that Zoe felt they already had played. She had even told her dad about the game while she was on a phone call with him. The next morning before the family left town, the mom stopped by the hospital and left a letter for Kayla. In it, she assured Kayla everything was fine and complimented Kayla's integrity. This letter included a check with instructions for Kayla to spend it on herself. This was indeed a moment when I was a proud parent, but it was really a God kiss, one of the positive memories from the hospital stay. Only God knows how that gesture moved in the other family, in Zoe, or in the staff who witnessed the gesture on both sides.

Scripture:

And we know that in all things God works for the good of those who love him, who have been called according to his purpose.

Romans 8:28

So whatever you wish that others would do to you, do also to them, for this is the Law and the Prophets.

Matthew 7:12

Carry each other's burdens, and in this way you will fulfill the law of Christ.

Galatians 6:2

LOVE Affirmed:

The golden rule truly is golden. Kayla witnessed and valued integrity, felt a sting when she perceived others lacked integrity, and wanted to set a good example for others. There is a reason we say she had a golden heart. Kayla, like each of us, was called according to God's purpose. This is true on the flip side of that comment as well. In other words God calling people according to a purpose can include helping you in your situation. It may even be a blessing to them to do so. Often people who are the most willing to help others are the least willing to accept help from others. If we are to do unto others we're also able to receive what others are willing to do unto us.

Plea from the Heart:

I am writing this entry on Kayla's second heavenly birthday. Perhaps one purpose for my writing this is something that is heavy on my heart in this moment and plan to release this book just after the second anniversary of her death. Before Kayla got sick, much of my time was given to my role as a caretaker in my mom's life. She needed help with everything pertaining to her self-care, and she needed help with her anxieties. I wrestled for a long while with letting others come in to help. I didn't allow it, and this caused more stress than necessary for many, Mom and myself included.

Mom lived with us, so when Kayla became sick and went to the hospital, my brother, sister-in-love, and niece moved into my house to take care of Haley and Mom. My Dad would pick up grocery orders and bring them to the house, and he came for reading dates with Haley and Madi. This allowed me to stay at the hospital, and allowed Dustin, my husband, to divide his time between work, the hospital, and home. This help made sense. I had no trouble accepting this help. And I remain forever grateful for it.

A point came when Kayla made great progress. It was possible that she'd be discharged from the hospital. My extended family and church family heard this and asked about my greatest concerns and needs. Our farmhouse had carpet that we had not replaced since buying the home more than 15 years earlier. Bringing Kayla home with the old carpet would not have been an option, and we would need to change bed sheets daily because of her immune system.

My family heard this need and purchased many sheet sets. Financial help also came from many directions. My church facilitated replacing our carpet with flooring that was easier to sanitize. Had Kayla been well enough, home was ready for her. This help was harder to accept. The pride monster gets funny sometimes. But with urging, we accepted because it was for Kayla and her health.

After Kayla passed, followed closely by Mom's dwindling health and passing, I felt a deep change. I felt as if I were in a hole and had no clue how to get out. I couldn't even pray. I could only be around a few close family members and friends—otherwise, I knew if I remained in this hole, not only was I a detriment to myself but also to others around me.

I kept, and sometimes still keep, an emotional arm's length between myself and others. Nothing short of a helpful hand, a whole lot of prayer, and the Holy Spirit through those around me, would help me get out. I was sad. This wasn't sadness. This wasn't grieving. This was numbness. Being stuck. Back-pedaling. Facing flashbacks. Restlessness. Inconsolable tears and anger. This was not my character, and this was not okay. If I remained in this hole, not only was I a detriment to myself but also to others.

I needed help. I needed to model what getting help looked like. This kind of help, specifically the help of a professional counselor, did not make sense at first and was honestly the hardest to accept. Pridefully, I felt needing a counselor or a medication was my faith falling short. But as I write this that pride has been humbled. I recognize now God is at work through the medication and counseling. Seeking help and accepting help is not a lack of faith. Rather, it is a tool He Himself made available for my healing.

God is the Wonderful Counselor. Through the Holy Spirit in us and in others, God will work situations for the good of those called according to His purpose. While loved ones, prayers, counselors, and therapists can help with many things, in my case, PTSD, they are powerless if we do not admit our need for accepting help. Please, I urge you, if you feel stuck, like you are back-pedaling, or perhaps like you are drowning, please consider seeking and accepting help.

Prayer:

Thank You that You are the I AM. Thank You that You know the needs of Your chosen. Thank You that we have an example to follow and imitate—yes, through Jesus but also through Jesus in faith-filled followers. Lord, I pray that if anyone has a need for help that they will be overcomers. May they have enough faith that they are able to move the mountain of whatever stands between them and that help—fear, doubt, pride, judgmental people, whatever that maybe. Let them take Your hand and begin healing by deciding to, and following through on, seeking help today.

Smiles to Share – Section 2

Help

I found myself at sunrise, overlooking water on a pier,
Just beyond the boughs of a weeping willow tree, with lots of
wildlife near.
Often when I'm out alone like this, I'll play a silent game;
I try to be there without disturbing what was there when I came.
An egret perched upon the rail, two squirrels ate at the base of a tree,
and fifteen deer just grazed, all aware but without care of me.
Then as I gazed across the water, letting go of fear, doubt, and worry
in prayer,
a pair of cardinals joined me; they sat, flittered, and stared.
I wondered what they were thinking when they investigated me,
with tears silently flowing near the weeping willow tree.

God, help this selfish sinner, often, my problems seem bigger than
You.
Help me walk forgiven and treat others how I'd like them to treat me
too.
When there is so much more to say, Lord, You know how to reach
Your own.
Thank You for reminding me that I don't have to hurt alone.
There are people out there blessed and equipped to lend a hand.
God remind me it's okay to ask and accept help, help me understand.
Thank You for your creation, Lord; its beauty and refreshment too.
Thank You for Your forgiveness, when I fall short in what I do.

Connecting Ideas:
1) A weeping willow is a tree. If you could make a tree look any way you wanted, what would it look like?
2) What is your favorite quiet game to play?
3) Do you like the sunrise or the sunset better? Why?
4) Do you feel alone sometimes? Do you like feeling alone?
5) Sometimes people talk about a Golden Rule. The Golden Rule is that you should treat others the way you would want them to treat you.

So whatever you wish that others would do to you, do also to them, for this is the Law and the Prophets.
Matthew 7:12

6) Can you think of other things to talk about?

(Check out www.supposewithrose.com for free downloadable coloring pages or activities.)

God Is Always Chasing After You

Three
The Truth

Dear Reader,

The Mary Poppins song, "A Spoon Full of Sugar," indeed maybe a catchy tune but it is a fictional concept, especially as it relates to truth. I have always had the privilege of being around people who spoke with direct truth. I experienced very little sugar coating in my life while I was growing up to "help the medicine go down." While that seemed harsh sometimes, I actually wouldn't have had it any other way. I focus on that same kind of truth for my kiddos, family, and friends—or at least I aim to. The fact is, people can typically tell if someone is lying or if something isn't right about the story, or if a story isn't complete.

Funny enough, a similar story happened to both of my children several years apart. A classmate of each girl told her that their pet fish changed colors and grew after the child had given the fish a bath with soap. Each classmate said the fish was found "sleeping" at the top of its aquarium.

Both Kayla and Haley knew the kind of fish being described did not change colors, nor did they sleep with their bellies up. Kayla responded, "Mom, why did their parents lie to them?" and Haley responded, "I don't feel safe with my friend's mother anymore."

What seems like an innocent fib meant to protect someone may well set that person up for hard times when bigger problems come along—not to mention that parents should set the example showing lying is not acceptable.

One of the hardest questions I had to field while raising my daughters was whether or not their grandma, my mom, was going to die. I had been Mom's caretaker all during my daughters' young lives. When we purchased our home, we intentionally designated a corner of the house for Mom. She was oxygen dependent, a high stroke risk, and typically, had at least one trip to the emergency room every year with pneumonia admissions, which would become more often and longer over time.

So, when my children asked if Grandma was going to be okay, the honest answer for them was, "I don't know. None of us are promised the next moment here. Remember if we know Jesus, just because we aren't alive in our body here doesn't mean we aren't healed in Heaven."

This opened the door for even harder questions, including one that I pray is the hardest I'll ever experience. Kayla, in her ICU bed, woke in a panic. "Momma, what if I die?"

Startled awake, I asked her to repeat her question. I was honestly hoping I'd misheard. I grabbed my bedside stool and pulled it next to her to hold her hand while we spoke. She repeated her question. Fear rattled from the pit of her being, and her eyes were so wide as the tears falling were like a riptide carrying her further away from peace.

"Momma, what if I die?"

I took a big breath to try to somewhat contain my emotions. I prayed a quick prayer for God to be with me and give me His words. Her concern was so valid. She had learned well the lesson we are not promised tomorrow here.

"My child, what if you do?"

The following silence was a time of surrender and held such suspense in my soul. I wanted to give her that "spoon full of sugar," but sugar wouldn't help. She needed to know the truth.

"I know Jesus."

"Yes! What else?"

"I know He prepared a place for me." She paused, "I know, death is not goodbye. It's 'See you later.'"

"Yes Darling. That's right."

She quickly followed her sigh of relief with another hard hitter: "Momma, I know I'll be okay, but what about y'all? Will y'all be okay?"

I held her hand tightly and stared in her eyes, now a dimmed blue as illness even affected them. My mind repeated, *Lord give me the strength, Lord I need words. Oh, Heaven help me.*

This silence felt even longer, it was as though she turned the tables on me. She needed to know I knew the truth, too.

In that moment, I felt every prayer that had been prayed over my family.

"Honey, if God sees fit to call you home, we will hurt big. But Love will get us through."

Kayla found peace in hearing this statement. Her demeanor became peaceful and calm. In that moment, my mind felt like an inflated balloon that was let go before it was tied. My heart and the Holy Spirit within me contained the frenzy—barely.

Kayla knew my confidence and my strength rested in the Lord. It wasn't in her ability to fight. It wasn't in her ability to heal. It wasn't in my ability to take care of her. It wasn't in the doctors or nurses or other support staff. Everything rested on God's will for Kayla, and ultimately, His promises for our lives.

As we often did, we said Psalm 23 together then sang "Amazing Grace." She drifted off into slumber, worn out from the gravity of emotions yet tucked in by the healing power of hope.

My nerves quaked. The nurse was in the room the entire time and witnessed all we said to each another. I slept at my "station" on the footstool, holding Kayla's hand for the rest of the night. The nurse had given me a rolled towel to use as a pillow since I didn't want to move. I quietly soaked the rolled towel with my eyes' "leaking" so I wouldn't disrupt Kayla's bedding or wounds. I was praying this conversation wasn't the Holy Spirit using my child to foreshadow events to come, yet I knew I needed His strength for whatever was coming.

Scripture:

Sorrow is better than laughter: for by the sadness of the countenance the heart is made better.
Ecclesiastes 7:3 (KJV)

"Let not your heart be troubled; you believe in God believe also in Me. In My Father's house are many mansions; if it were not so, I would have told you. I go to prepare a place for you."
Jesus speaking, John 14: 1–2 (KJV)

For the Spirit God gave us does not make us timid, but gives us power, love and self-discipline.
2 Timothy 1:7

LOVE Affirmed:

Truth, even when it is sorrowful, is the best approach when answering questions. At the time of her diagnosis, Kayla was 13. Haley was 9. Kayla and Haley both knew life, as we know it here, results in the death of our physical body eventually. They also knew we were being honest when we said Kayla was either going to be healed here or in Heaven.

I believe this truth helped all of us in every part of our process. The girls had the ability to trust us. We had the ability to be honest. They had the opportunity to understand through asking questions. We all had the opportunity to love to the fullest of our ability. I've come to cherish that moment with Kayla, tears and all. Had I tried to divert the sorrow or sugarcoat the truth, I wouldn't have had such a direct means to know my child's heart, because she knew she could share with me, too.

But what of those who have passed, and we do not know their hearts? For children, I remember, and find comfort to know, the baby in Elizabeth's womb leaped for joy (Luke 1:44) even before his birth, and Jesus himself rebuked those who tried to keep children from him.

The innocence of a child or infant leads me to believe his or her knowledge of Jesus is essentially unchanged yet by the world. For those who are not children, who perhaps are unable to express this reliance upon the Lord due to physical or emotional limitations, we lean on the Lord and His faithfulness, patience, and love. Remember on the cross of crucifixion, Jesus said to the thief, "Truly I tell you, today you will be with me in paradise." (Luke 23:43)

Many people I know who have been unconscious, have expressed an ability to know what is going on. If they have any form of awareness, who am I to assume God cannot reach them? Our confidence must rest on the Lord, come what may.

Is it up to the person to choose? Yes. Can I choose for them? No, but I can pray. A person's salvation and sanctification is the most intimate relationship in his or her life. A person may not have the opportunity to tell others about it. It is the desire of Jesus Christ, the Holy Spirit, and our Heavenly Father that we come to God, so I must rest assured that God will do all He can to reach a person and give him or her the opportunity to choose His love. Through time of intimate prayer, the Helper will offer His guidance in sharing Truth as I go in this life. My responsibility is to walk heeding this guidance and resting in Truth.

Prayer:

Lord, You're the same yesterday, today, and tomorrow; we are not. We grow, learn, and change. Father, there isn't a smidge of judgment here. I pray truth be considered as a gift. At the same time, Lord, You tell us to not allow our hearts to be troubled. You tell us to focus on things above and keep our thoughts captive to You and on praiseworthy things.

In times such as these, trust feels more fragile than thin glass that will shatter if even one pebble gets thrown. May Your Word be a refuge. Wrap each reader in love and truth, Lord, no matter his or her struggles. In a way only Your Holy Spirit through Our Lord and Savior Jesus Christ can, help this reader face their feelings by standing firm in faith and in Your faithfulness.

Something's Fishy

Monday, Mom and Dad had work. I had school and got to learn and play. That night, we had catfish we'd caught on the weekend for dinner. It was a normal day.

Mom asked, "Did you brush your teeth and take care of 'bathroom biz?'" I told her I did, But when she came to tuck me in, she smelled my breath and said, "Something's fishy kid."

When Mom gave me the look, I knew more than the fish got caught. Mom and Dad hoped I'd learned to stop lying, but my actions showed I had not.

After consequences, Mom made me brush my teeth and say sorry, you see. She said God, the Father, wants only truth for me.

Wednesday, the nurse had a needle to give me a shot. I asked if it was going to hurt. The nurse told me, "No, it would not."

I said, "Something's fishy kid." Mom smiled and looked me in the eye, "It will hurt some for a little while, but it's okay if you cry.

I can wrap you in a hug, hold your hand, and we can pray. My child, I can promise God is with us, and because He is love, we will be okay."

My Dad asked later about my day. I told him I did not like the shot. But said, "The worst part was I wanted to believe the nurse, but she lied, so I could not."

I asked Dad what the reason people tell "fishy stories" is. He told me it could be people don't like the consequences. Or maybe they don't like the hard feelings truth sometimes brings.

But he said, "The truth, even if it is hard and hurts, sets you free from many things." "Don't they know they can hold a hand and pray?" I asked. "Don't they know because God is love, He is with them and it will be okay?"

"My child," Dad said while he smiled, "May you remain wise beyond your fears. I pray you always know God is with you through the years."

Turns out there is nothing "fishy" about the truth, it just is what it is. Mom and Dad taught me God says being honest if part of being a child of His.

Friends, as years go by, almost nothing stays the same. Even you will change, but Love never does. That's why Love is my favorite God name.

Connecting Ideas:
1)   Have you ever felt something slimy? Tell me that story!
2)   Have you ever gone fishing? Did you like it? Why or why not?
3)   Do you like the story? What is your favorite or least favorite part? Why?
4)   How does it make you feel if someone lies to you?
(If you are talking with a young child, you may need to explain lie and truth. "If I said there was a green pig sitting on my nose, is that truth or a lie? It may be silly, but really it is a lie, because there is not a green pig on my nose.")
5)   Sometimes we have to tell the truth even if we are afraid. Telling the truth is one way to love others. The Bible tells us:

For the Spirit God gave us does not make us timid, but gives us power, love and self-discipline.
2 Timothy 1:7

6)   Can you think of anything else you want to talk about or ask?

(Check out www.supposewithrose.com for free downloadable coloring pages or activities.)

Four
Shine Friend, Shine

Dear Reader,

I recall well a trip to school one morning when Kayla made a rather profound statement. "I don't get the idea of pretty. If everyone knew what someone else has been through, they'd see what beauty really is."

She did not understand the fuss her classmates made over appearances. Not long after this, COVID-19 struck, and many of these social situations and pressures were put on hold. I consider this, in our situation, a protection for Kayla.

During our first stent in the ICU, I found Kayla looking at herself in the restroom mirror. "Mom, I don't know that girl, I don't like how she looks," she said.

Her outward appearance had indeed changed. Her eyes were darker, face and skin wrought with rash, and overall, she just showed her sickness. She had cut her hair so when it began to fall out, the hair loss wouldn't be as drastic to watch. But more importantly in that reflective moment, her countenance dropped. For the first time in her life, Kayla looked at her outward self and wished it looked different.

"Remember, God doesn't look at our appearances, so we do not look at our appearances or our circumstances to define who we are either. God looks to the hidden person of the heart," I said.

We spoke about how she was created in the image of God. That He knew she had been praying for those around her and those who were caring for her. God knew instead of complaining about how bad she felt, she simply informed nurses what was going on with her body and tried her best to focus on things she could do instead of things she couldn't.

"And that," I put my hands on her cheeks and stepped between her and the mirror, "is a beautiful and strong girl, shining the light of Jesus into the world."

We finished all the business she had to do in the bathroom, including the daily head-to-toe body wipes and the medicated mouthwash, and re-entered the room. Apparently, our conversation had caught the nurse's attention, too, and she had been listening in. The nurse was visibly shaken and asked if what I was saying was true.

"Yes, ma'am." I responded and Kayla nodded as she settled into bed. "I would have to look up the verses, but I can assure you it's all in Scripture." I joked that I may have a good imagination, but this time I didn't make anything up.

A deep silence surrounded us over the next several minutes as the nurse and I put ice packs around Kayla's body to bring down her fever. Once Kayla drifted into a medicine-induced sleep, the nurse told me how helpful those words would have been if she had heard them sooner. And she complimented me on being a good mom; I told her those words didn't come from me or my ability but from the Holy Spirit through the Bible.

Scripture:

All scripture is God-breathed and is useful for teaching, rebuking, correcting, and training in righteousness, so that the servant of God may be thoroughly equipped for every good work.
2 Timothy 3:16–17

"The LORD does not look at the things people look at. People look at the outward appearance, but the LORD looks at the heart."
1 Samuel 16:7

As iron sharpens iron, so one person sharpens another.
Proverbs 27:17

Love Affirmed:

As we live out who we are in Christ, the Holy Spirit works around, in, and through us. Kayla was surprised by the nurses' questions. Our pastor had once commented that we are all on a mission to share the gospel with everyone we meet, that we are all missionaries at every moment just by the way we live our lives. That day, she understood his comment. I think Kayla originally felt mission work looked like telling people more directly about who Jesus is and what He has done, rather than simply living out our identity in Christ.

From that time forward, we made a point to remember who God is by referencing different names for Him. We also made a point to remember who He says we are. One game we played was a hand game Haley and I'd made up two years before, claiming things God calls us. (Read Smiles to Share God's Child for the words.)

Everyone can benefit from learning just who we are in Christ. Chosen and called by name for a purpose. Beautiful, as we are His workmanship and masterpiece. His actions and sacrifice show us we are worthy of His love because of His love. We are dearly loved children who can call Him Father journeying on a path together and blessed He would tell us any part of His plan and allow us to say we are a friend.

Prayer:

Adonai (ad-o-noy), which means "Lord our Master," You are *El Shaddai* (el shad-di), which means Lord God Almighty. You are *Abba,* or "Daddy," and present in our lives so we can know You as *Jehovah Jireh* (yeh-ho-vaw yir-eh) or "the Lord will provide." We call on You as *Jehovah Rapha* (yeh-ho-vaw raw-faw), "the Lord that Heals." No matter where we are along this journey of healing, Father we place our faith in You. May we walk in step with the purpose You have for our lives, that You may be lifted higher—higher than the world around us; higher than our circumstances; higher than our understanding—that we may approach each day with peace. If it be Your will, Father, allow us be a beacon for You, living as if to hear You saying, "Shine Child, Shine."

God's Child

I've been called so many things since the breath of life was breathed into me.
Of course, the first names I remember were given by my family.

Then there are the pet names I'm called some of the time.
These names are kind of silly and are names I don't mind.

But somehow as I've gotten older, and I really don't know why.
People start using names to bully; they make me feel bad maybe even cry.

I'm told to ignore them. I'm told that, "Words can never hurt."
But the truth is they do sometimes. They can make me feel like dirt.

The worst names, however, are the ones I say inside to myself.
I cannot imagine how much trouble I'd be in if I said them to someone else.

I don't know why I do that, why I say mean names.
But I know it helps to know what God calls me, the ones He proclaims.

So,
I open the Holy Bible
To put these things (or my fears) to bed, bed, bed.
I asked God what He calls me, and this is what He said, said, said;

God calls me:
"Chosen" (by name),
"Beautiful,"
"Masterpiece,"
"Worthy,"
"Purposed,"
"Dearly beloved,"
"Treasure."
God calls me:
"Chosen" (by name),
"Beautiful,"
"Masterpiece,"
"Worthy,"
"Purposed,"
"Dearly beloved,"
"Treasure."
God calls me "Friend!"

There are other names God calls me, too, like strong, overcomer, and unique
These names help me remember His are the names I should seek!

So, I decided when the things I'm called make me feel like I should frown.
I will choose to remember what God calls me, to turn my frown upside down.

Below are the names listed in the song and a point of reference for them in Scripture. Some have many more points of reference in Scripture than those listed. Open a Bible and see if you can find them. Perhaps you can use one of these verses to turn a frown upside down—yours or one of your friends'!

Chosen (By Name)- 1 Peter 2:9

Masterpiece (Ephesians 2:10)

Purposed (Romans 8:28)

Treasure. (Deuteronomy 7:6)

Strong (2 Timothy 1:7)

Unique (Psalm 139:13)

Beautiful (Ecclesiastes 3:11)

Worthy (Exodus 14:14)

Dearly Beloved (1 John 4:11)

Friend (John 15:15)

Overcomer (John 16:33)

Connecting Ideas:
1)   Did you know you can turn part of this story into a hand game? Try it! Pick three moves or come up with your own. Repeat them over and over while you say the part starting at, "I open the Holy Bible," and hug yourself when you say, "God calls me friend."
   a. Clap your hands together.
   b. Tap your hands on your legs.
   c. Clap hands with someone else.
   d. Fist bump.
   e. Twinkle your fingers.
2)   Are you called any silly names? Did your name just get picked or was there a reason you were given your real name or a silly name?
3)   Is there a name in the story you like best? Maybe one that might help you turn a frown upside down?
4)   Are there times you call yourself mean names inside? When do you do that most?
5)   We can help each other, and God wants us to. The Bible says:

As iron sharpens iron, so one person sharpens another.
Proverbs 27:17

6) Can you think of other things to talk about?

God Is Always Chasing After You

Five
Mighty Miracle

Dear Reader,

During our storms, it was hard to witness the success stories, or the miracles, if you will, of others around us. It is simply human nature to ask, "Why not me?"

This was also true for my tenderhearted Kayla, myself, and others in our family. This question still visits my thoughts on hard days, and I am sure that will be the case until I am before my Maker in Glory. Please understand, this isn't an ill wish for others. It's more like a position or place along the grieving trail, where expectations and reality didn't line up.

Realistically, it is a layer of envy. Just as coveting another's car is envy, so is desiring another's health.   And, in our flesh-covered experience, we must mention this, even if it stings to admit. Envy is like a slippery slope and can single-handedly slide you and your loved ones into a sorrowful space. In my opinion and experience, it's best to take that envy in hand, or that bull by the horns if you will. But how?

When we found ourselves with "Why not . . . " thoughts, looking at the good in someone else's life verses the struggle of our own, I challenged Kayla and myself to think of our own mighty miracles. We read of them in Scripture. We reflected on those we'd seen and experienced in our lives and in the lives of people we know and love. One miracle that carried us is Miracle, the little bull calf.

Our family lives on a farm. This was one of the greatest joys my daughter Kayla and my mom, Debra, had in their lives. They loved animals. I'll admit the farm is a treasure chest of wonderful memories, but for me, it is more a series of often-difficult tasks to complete, with hard life lessons.

One morning before Kayla's illness overtook our actions and moments, Kayla discovered an expectant cow down. Daisy had somehow wrapped herself in barbed wire. Kayla rallied the troops of the farm. After a few pulled muscles, scrapes, and scratches, we had Daisy unwrapped, but down she remained. She required special attention.

We had to feed, clean, water, shift, even helped her to stand, and give antibiotics—multiple tasks, multiple times daily. Work to some. Joy to Kayla and Mom. At this point Mom couldn't get out of the house, but her coaching and wisdom ran our little farm especially in times like this.

For three weeks, this special attention continued—until one of those hard life lessons entered. Daisy was not going to heal, but she was still pregnant with an active calf making itself known with strong kicks and belly flips. So, all those farm troops rallied again. Daisy was relieved of her suffering, and we delivered a very tiny bull calf later named Miracle.

Before she even spoke, Kayla's eyes begged us to make raising this boy her special project. (This wasn't our cow or calf, but Kayla's aunt and uncle didn't mind if we made the attempt to nurture him.) I hesitated. First, premature animals rarely survive; this calf was at least six weeks, if not eight, early. Second, it was the wet wintertime. The only way to give this baby what he needed would be to raise him in the house. And last, my caretaking plate was full.

But I prayed and ended up saying, "Yes." Not only did Miracle survive, but also his presence made the last Christmas our family had with Kayla, Mom, and Great Aunt Gloria one of great memories and joys—poo-cans, pee-cans, drench feeds, laughs, and all. This calf would stumble through the living room and hallway, Kayla following with a can or cup in each hand, just in case, and our farm coach, her grandma, beaming all the while.

Our experience with Miracle, that tiny bull calf was something we pulled on, knowing all he went through, yet he survived. In the few and far between times when Kayla felt like giving up, or experienced great sorrow, she had the life lessons of the farm and the testimony of Mighty Miracle to draw on.

For example one encounter with great sadness centered on Kayla's desire to be a mom. With the initial chemo, it would still have been possible for her to have children someday. But after the be procedure to prepare her body for stem cell transplant, motherhood would no longer an option.

This hurt could have brought deep despair. Instead, we chose to recollect just how much joy Kayla had in caring for animals. She even had a photo album, her animal book, she proudly shared. Kayla experienced the joy of giving unconditional love—just rather than two-legged smooth skinned babies, hers all had four feet or feathers.

Scripture:

Finally, brothers and sisters, whatever is true, whatever is noble, whatever is right, whatever is pure, whatever is lovely, whatever is admirable—if anything is excellent or praiseworthy—think about such things.
Philippians 4:8

The LORD himself goes before you and will be with you; he will never leave you nor forsake you. Do not be afraid; do not be discouraged."
Deuteronomy 31:8

So then, just as you received Christ Jesus as Lord, continue to live your lives in him, rooted and built up in him, strengthened in the faith as you were taught, and overflowing with thankfulness.
Colossians 2: 6–7

LOVE Affirmed:

When I ponder all the moving pieces, I cannot deny the Father's hand at work in life. Even in the hurtful times. When we know God is in the details of our lives, little blessings encourage and empower us and allow us to experience the blessing of a grateful heart.

As mentioned, it was hard to witness the miracles around us during our storm and loss—especially if we took our eyes off our own miracles. I believe it is important to recall a "miracle" or amazing happening you witnessed, if possible, involving or with the one you love who is ill.

Frankly, every one of us is a miracle and defies odds and statistics. Recall the emotions of the amazing miracle moments, however small they may seem. Praise God for your miracle. Let it serve as a reminder. Tell that story to others, even if you share it a thousand times. Finding the praiseworthy, even amid the sorrow, is a gift the Holy Spirit can give you as you walk through the hardest of days. Finding the good can offer footing when you feel you're on slippery slopes of grief or discouragement.

Some may scoff, and question, "Really? How? What does that look like?"

I think of one grateful comment from Kayla, when her feet were too swollen even to fit in the oversized slippers and she wore sunglasses because the light intensified the nasty chemo induced headache. She said, "Thank You God for squirrels," referring to the little rodents running races around the park outside. Their game of chase made her giggle. In their own way, these squirrels helped take Kayla's mind off the pain even if only for moments at a time and in that moment they were all she could find to say thank you about.

Often a grateful moment for my mom, who was anxiety ridden and "tied," she felt, to the oxygen machine, was when she could say, "I was able to do the dishes today. Thanks God." The days she contributed to the home, she felt, were good days.

"Thanks, Otter Box!" was a point of humor and gratitude from Dustin, since who knows how many times I dropped my cell phone while slipping into a doze, exhausted in every way possible. Without that Otter Box my phone surely would have shattered.

Finding the good can give us footing on the steep slopes surrounding the healing journey. Like bighorn sheep scaling mountainsides, we must watch where we place ourselves. Thankfully we need not bust heads together with the other sheep. Instead, we can heed the voice of our Heavenly Father regarding where to step.

Prayer:
Father, forgive me. I recall days when I felt there was nothing to be thankful for. At some points, even praising you for the fact that Kayla was alive felt selfish, Lord, as her pain and suffering was so intense. But my actions do not surprise You, just like the Reader's actions do not surprise you. Thank You for your instruction on what

to meditate on, Lord. We praise you for all the life we live here—every single moment.

Thank You for the person reading this—this one's life and the lives of those the reader's life touches. You alone know this person's story with the biggest picture there is. May the "mighty miracles' in the readers' lives become clear. May they experience the power of a grateful heart as they journey through stormy times and fix their eyes on you.

Smiles to Share – Section 5

Psalm 23

There is a girl I know, Kayla is her name.
Kayla called out to her Creator as each day came.
No matter her struggle she presented a grateful heart.
Matter of fact, "Thank you," was how her prayers would start.
Some days she only prayed before eating food.
On others, how and when she prayed depended on her mood.
But friends, there were times Kayla did not know what to pray.
Times she found not having words was okay.
She learned how comforting praying Scripture could be.
So, she decided to pray Psalm twenty-three.
~

The Lord is my shepherd;
I shall not want.
He makes me to lie down in green pastures;
He leads me beside the still waters.
He restores my soul;
He leads me in the paths of righteousness
For His name's sake.
Yea, though I walk through the valley of the shadow of death,
I will fear no evil;
For You are with me;
Your rod and Your staff, they comfort me.
You prepare a table before me in the presence of my enemies;
You anoint my head with oil;

God Is Always Chasing After You

My cup runs over.
Surely goodness and mercy shall follow me
All the days of my life;
And I will dwell in the house of the Lord Forever.

Psalm 23 (NKJV)

If ever you find you don't know what words to say.
Know just being silent in prayer is okay.
Perhaps you'll find praying Scripture meaningful too.
May you learn more about Jesus and all He did (and still does) for you.
I hope, dear friend, like Kayla, you can grow to see.
How helpful a grateful heart, or just saying, "thank you," can be.

Connecting Ideas:

1)   Tell me what you know about sheep? Or do you know a story about them?

("Ba-Ba black Sheep," "Mary had a Little Lamb," "Old McDonald")

2)   Let's talk about something that feels soft. What is your favorite soft thing?

3)   Do you like when everything is quiet around you? Why or why not?

4)   Have you ever not known what to say or what to pray? When?

5)   This story talked about a grateful heart or saying, "Thank you." If you keep what Jesus did for you in your heart, thankfulness can overflow. The Bible says:

> *So then, just as you received Christ Jesus as Lord, continue to live your lives in him, rooted and built up in him, strengthened in the faith as you were taught, and overflowing with thankfulness.*
> **Colossians 2: 6–7**

6) Can you think of other things to talk about, or do you have questions to ask?

(Check out www.supposewithrose.com for free downloadable coloring pages or activities.)

Six
Wonder Wanders

Dear Reader,

Another difficult factor when you have a person sick, no matter at the hospital or at home, for an extended time is balancing relationships. In regard to long term chronic medical needs, often those who are not ill feel they're missing out on the love of the caretaker. This was sometimes the case for our family in reference to my Mom's health needs long before Kayla became ill. Once Kayla became ill this missing out feeling intensified as we had a child at the hospital and a child at home. We were blessed. We had family nearby to step in and help meet our caretaking needs. But the tension undoubtedly created obstacles in our parent/child relationships. Not to mention the marriage relationship or those relationships of close friends and family.

From my daughter Haley's perspective, I went from being the mom who'd never leave my children with anyone, including family, for more than a night at a time, to spending 124 consecutive days away from her physically, not to mention the time after Kayla's death when I walked in a daze and was emotionally unattached in my grief. From Haley's perspective, frankly, Kayla and I had abandoned her.

Sure, she understands why as well as she can, and she wouldn't have asked me to do anything differently. She appreciated our talks and times together. But her feelings and perspectives are valid and are hers to feel. It takes great grace to remember a person's feelings aren't a personal attack. Nor are their feelings yours to carry. Rather they are their experiences. They're evidence of their perspective, and their perspective and feelings are valid. My experience wasn't Haley's experience to understand.

Similarly, initially, Mom in her illness struggled with feeling abandoned. Sometimes, even in our own grief, we must model unconditional love. In this situation, just as deeply as I needed to connect with God, personally, my child and my mom, needed to connect with me. Finding ways of connecting with others, including children, may take some creativity. That's difficult enough to do sometimes, even in normal everyday life. Add a critically or chronically ill loved ones care as factor to the mix, or the emotions surrounding loss, and even more effort may be warranted.

On Sundays, Dustin would bring Haley to the hospital. Without special permission, and the best of clinical circumstances, the hospital personnel didn't recommend Kayla have visitors besides parents. Dustin would visit so Kayla could have Daddy time while I had a visit with Haley for Mommy time. During one of these visits, we met Wonder the Wandering Squirrel. He was just one of many squirrels, I am sure, but on this particular day, Wonder was acting especially bold, coming closer to Haley to retrieve the nuts I had given her to feed the little creature. This was a shared experience, uniquely ours, and one I cherish.

Haley went to the green area between a breezeway and a parking lot and knelt next to a tree. "Okay reach out but don't move any further, let the little dude decide how close to come," I instructed.

Wonder the Squirrel retreated behind a beam at the edge of the parking garage for a second but peeped back around either side of it to check his surroundings. Inch by inch, it seemed, he moved closer. *Step. Step. Freeze.* Run back a little, then toward Haley. Finally, Haley dropped a nut, and he came to get it so close she could touch him. I was proud of her for resisting.

"See how Wonder looks all around. That's how I feel Momma. I feel like I have to keep looking all around every step because I am afraid, and I don't know what is coming because you and Kayla aren't with me." Haley's comment broke my heart and made me realize I had to do something more to connect with her.

In our case, Haley was given a phone and was allowed to call me whenever she needed to. This helped her feel like she had a direct line to me, and she knew I'd answer, unless I absolutely could not—even if I was in the bathroom.

Sometimes it was just, "Mom I finished my ELA." Or, "Mom I made a smoothie for breakfast." Other times, I listened to the recount of her day or her thoughts. I'd say the trickiest task was explaining long division via video chat.

All kidding aside, throughout all phases of this experience, I believe it was not only essential that little connections continued, but crucial that we developed, valued, and validated an understanding and appreciation for each other's different perspectives, personalities, and experiences. Much like our Heavenly Father values and validates each of us.

Scripture:

Then he (Jesus) said to them all: "Whoever wants to be my disciple must deny themselves and take up their cross daily and follow me.
Luke 9:23

"For my thoughts are not your thoughts, neither are your ways my ways," declares the LORD.
Isaiah 55: 8

LOVE Affirmed:

Recognizing where control rests matters, but so does perspective.

I was thankful for Wonder the Squirrel and his anxious little self. He was a great representation of how we live, especially when we feel we are in control. The squirrel is one of God's creatures that must push comfort and boundaries for mere survival. Another thing this little rodent reminded me was that I couldn't control much of anything—neither could anyone else—and having even one thing we can control helps.

Wonder the Squirrel was in control of the approach to the prize, even if he used an approach I would not have taken, it was his approach, not Haley's. Likewise, I'm in control of my choice and actions. For example, the choice of taking up the cross daily is in my control, as is true for each of us who seek to follow Jesus, no matter our circumstance. Often choices we make are driven greatly by perspective.

God Is Always Chasing After You

"What can I control about this situation?" I often asked myself, and the answer usually was, "Very little." One vital fact to remember was the Lord went before. Another question was, "What control can Kayla, Haley, or Dustin have."

Bedding changes during the last ICU days were very uncomfortable for Kayla, these made her realize how much she could not do for herself. During these times, Dustin respected and protected her privacy, remembering to shut the curtains and keep her covered. She appreciated his protection. I'd place a wipe in her hand so she could clean herself. As limited as this was, it was something she could do, and gave her a tiny element of feeling in control of an aspect of her life. Even if during the final days rhabdomyolysis had robbed her of any significant bodily movement her holding the wipes made her feel like she was assisting in her own care.

For Haley, the phone gave her control of reaching out, and this helped her feel connected, though we were apart. For Dustin, having the option to come stay at the hospital between shifts offered him choice and opened the door for him to make sure I was trying to take care of myself while I cared for Kayla.

This idea of recognizing control and perspective remains true following the loss of our loved ones. At the time of this books writing, our family is approaching two years after Kayla's death. Some people carry the perspective, "It's time for you to get back to normal." Or perhaps they are in a place where they compare grief and the come off as a bit dismissive to our loss. It has helped for us to remember others do not hold our perspective, frankly, they can't. Each individual is in control of our own actions and approach.

Readers, comments or even self-expectations may come and wreak havoc on hearts and reveal the commentor's own hurt or inexperience. Comments that seem to try to compare grief or that carry a step you may not be ready for. May I remind you, there truly is only an audience of One. You have control over who you allow to influence your heart. The One. Only God, and His leading through the Holy Spirit, matters. When a person is grieving either the loss of a loved one or an unmet expectation, people often fail to pray—or sometimes even think—before they speak. While silence is a salve that speaks empathy and understanding, society has trained us to feel

54

silence is awkward. Don't let another person's past hurt or lack of perspective—and their response to your experience—hinder your healing. Lean instead on the healing made available through God and His promises.

Prayer:

Lord, we are Your creation. You know our anxious hearts and how desperately they yearn to be able to understand and control factors that are Yours to control. May we always remember that we have control over our choices, even if these choices are limited and not ones we would have desired for ourselves or our loved ones. Help us remember to focus on what we can do and can have, rather than focusing on that which we cannot do or have.

Help us remember that You chose us before we chose You. You chose us to walk this experience through either Your active or Your passive will. Ours is not to know, control, or even understand it all. But it is comforting to simply know that You know us to our core and still desire to connect with us deeply, despite our human nature—and even when the connection is through silent tears.

Smiles to Share – Section 6

Wonder the Wandering Squirrel

"He's a ball of fur. He's pretending to be a plane. And no one knows when he came. He's Wonder the Wandering Squirrel. Faster than a sprinting toddler. Sneakier too. You may never know if Wonder the Wandering Squirrel is watching you. Ready to grab your trail mix if you let him."

Mom's announcer voice trying a little comic relief and creating a character out of the squirrel in front of us.

I felt embarrassed by Mom's playful imagination. Mom always told me she wasn't shy, but until that moment, I really hadn't seen Mom let such silliness fly, especially with so many watching. I was on my weekly visit at the hospital where my sister Kayla had been for two months.

"Seriously Mom?" My cheeks felt as red as the shirt on my back, and I scrunched down as if to hide.

"Absolutely not. Now I'm Seriously." Mom shifted the mood, lowered her tone, and crossed her arms with a frown on her face to help me understand her drastic name change. Mom acted as though there was nothing to smile about in a playful way, and she waited. I knew what she was waiting for. And I knew she'd wait a long time.

I enjoyed the time Mom and I had, even if it had to be short. It helped me feel like Mom wanted to be with me and know how I was doing. It reminded me Mom cared even if we only had minutes together.

I swallowed hard. I was so concerned about the strangers watching us in the hospital walkway but then I noticed a tiny bird watching the squirrel closely and made her part of the story.

"Frederica Finch, that's my name, stealing Wonder the Wandering Squirrel's treats is my aim," I said in the highest-pitched sassy voice I could squeak out, and joined in Mom's game. Before long the statues, trees, and many more birds were part of our little pretend community. Mom's favorite voice of mine I turned into the wise country pigeon with a southern drawl.

"Come here son, I say, what you gotta do is," Mom's eyes were happy and surprised with the wise bird's advice.

When the pigeon landed as if to whisper a plan to gain the nuts Mom and I giggled for a good while. It was as though the pigeon recognized its part. We thought it was very funny.

When I saw Dad I knew my weekly visit with Mom was coming to a close and shifted to my best narrator voice, "Haley the Amazing scattered seed in order to save Wonder from the feisty feathered foes. Wonder the Wandering Squirrel worries no more thanks to his human hero." Then I spread the nuts from my trail mix out so Wonder the Wandering Squirrel could collect them.

Later, when I was home on a face-to-face call with Mom and my sister Kayla, I read a story with characters and used special voices just like Mom and I did earlier. Though Kayla could not say it, her smile showed me she enjoyed hearing my playful reading. I'm happy I helped my sister forget her pain enough to smile that day. I love and miss her so much.

Connecting Ideas:
1) Can you use something around us to pretend you are a superhero? What would your superpower be?
2) What would you do if you were a squirrel?
3) Do you like the story? What is your favorite part? Why?
4) How have you helped someone before?
5) In this story we hear about people-watching and making Haley nervous. Haley made a choice to stop worrying about the people watching. It help to remember God is in control and His opinion is the only one that matters. Scripture says:

Then he [Jesus] said to them all: "Whoever wants to be my disciple must deny themselves and take up their cross daily and follow me.
Luke 9:23

6) Can you think of anything else that you want to talk about or ask?

(Check out www.supposewithrose.com for free downloadable coloring pages or activities.)

Seven
A Feathery Reminder

Dear Reader,

Birds, all birds, big and small, have always caught my attention. Give it a beak and feathers, and I'm likely to take a second, third, or even tenth look. Maybe the birds look pretty. Their feathers resemble a rainbow of contrasting colors that cause me to remember God as a promise keeper (the first rainbow appeared as God's promise that the world would never be destroyed in a flood again). Maybe I like to watch birds because some species stay together for life. Their loyalty and faithfulness to their feathered life mate helps me to reminisce about the beauty of predictable relationships. Maybe they sing a pleasant song. The melody radiates a peaceful, carefree expression of the praise they sing to their Creator.

Sometimes I focus on birds for not-so-good ways. Perhaps they look frightening with their backward knees, slotted eyes, or their ability to turn their head backwards. Perhaps the bird is territorial and refuses to share its space, scaring others away. I've been attacked and or chased by a scissortail fly catcher, countless owls, hawks, roosters, turkeys, and even ostriches on a drive-thru animal experience.

By far the worst bird experience I can recall was when I was chased by a duck I call Mallard Drake. This guy had my cousins and me stuck in a pool. Claws on my cousins head at the other side of a shared float. Wings flapping and feathers flying. Even though my protective dad ended that threat, big emotions still circle that memory for all three of us cousins.

Recently, one summer day when it seemed as if popcorn popped itself in the summer heat, my family and I were visiting an amusement park. I didn't feel up to riding rides, so sightseeing was my activity while Haley and Dustin rode the rides. While I was taking a walk, a green-headed duck, or *Señor Pato la Cabeza Verde,* as I dubbed him joined. I spoke to him defensively, "Listen here

Señor Pato la Cabeza Verde, when I met your Great Uncle Mallard Drake, we got off on the wrong little orange foot."

As you can imagine, because of my history with Mallard Drake, I keep an eye on *Verde* as I read the signs telling me about statues and buildings. Bringing up the orange foot made me wonder what *Verde* would do if I poured some water on the pavement. It had to be hot. So I did. I couldn't let his rude uncle cloud my judgment on him, right? Of course not.

Verde, soft-spoken as he was, seemed to enjoy the cool spot and the conversation. He followed me, waddle and all, to four different places, I'd pour him a cool spot, and he waited on it patiently. We spoke while we walked. *Verde* even slipped a little joke in when he said he liked to quack around.

"Well, *Señor Pato la Cabeza Verde*, it's been fun waddling around together." I had come to a chapel. "It's time to part ways. I'm not sure how long I'll be in here, but it will surely be long enough for the pavement to heat back up on your little orange feet."

Verde, as though he understood fully, quacked a goodbye, waddled to a nearby pond, joined a group of ladies, and swam off to his ducky business. I entered the chapel and signed the visitor book. I penned a request in the prayer log for our grieving family and sat quietly in prayer. Amazed at just how God is in our every detail.

Scripture:

My intercessor is my friend as my eyes pour out tears to God; on behalf of a man he pleads with God as one pleads for a friend.
Job 16:20–21

Cast all your anxiety on him because he cares for you.
1 Peter 5:7

God Is Always Chasing After You

The Lord is close to the brokenhearted and saves those who are crushed in spirit.

Psalm 34:18

LOVE Affirmed:

Through the covering of Christ and His Holy Spirit, my quackish-speaking duck reminded me when we, or someone we love, prepare to go to the Father's house, we need to C- A- S- T. Yes, brothers and sisters, we must cast out our prayers, our hurts, our thoughts, our hope, to the Holy Spirit our Intercessor.

1) C- Continue forward. (Even if you have wings and can fly, at times a slow waddle is best.)

2) A- Accept the truth of what happened, or is happening, so you can be grateful for the time together.

3) S- Spend time with God. Remember your identity in Him.

4) T- Talk to God or His children around you. There's no benefit when you fly away from big emotions. It's okay to talk about your feelings; your feelings are valid.

Prayer:

Thank You Father. I love how You meet this mess and reassure me that You know me and all the details. My mind desires to understand the why and how, Lord. How can You know so much when I can barely remember what I walked into a room for at times? Why was this allowed to happen? But all that matters is what You can do, will do, or have done. If I am in Christ, there is no condemnation, as Your word says in Romans 8:1. Help us C-A-S-T cares and anxiety on You. Help us continue forward in Your time. Help us accept what is, so our grateful hearts may grow. Help us spend time with You in Your Word. Help us talk and connect with those You have placed in a position to help us know our feelings are heard and valid. Most of all, Lord, Help us find healing for our broken hearts.

Señor Pato la Cabeza Verde

A green-headed, orange-footed duck was swimming one summer day,
in a nice amusement parks pretty pond in the month of May.
He saw me watching him and his lady friends across the way.
He asked if he could walk with me; Oddly I said, "Yes, okay."
I named the duck, or Pato in Spanish, *Señor Pato la Cabeza Verde.*

Señor Pato la Cabeza Verde, he said what he'd say.
I imagined "I'm here," and "Thank you," in his quackish way.
I poured water on the ground for his feet that hot summer day.
At each stop I'd talk, he'd just listen, we'd look, and briefly stay.
He was nice to listen, not to make a scene and fly away.

You see I wasn't feeling happy, my mood was kind of gray.
I was missing someone who'd gone to be with Jesus to stay.
But God sent this duck to remind me, He's the perfect *Padre.*
He wants me to cast my cares on him—bad, or good, either way.
Even if they seem unreal like make believe or pretend play.

Thank you, for the time with my loved one, for every single day,
and for reminding me being happy and sad is okay.
Help me move forward in work, my memories, my school, and play.
You call the stars by name and still are big enough to hear me pray.
God You are love and You are with me, in every single way.

Connecting Ideas:
1) Do you know any words in Spanish or another language? Can you count?
2) What is your favorite place to visit?
3) Do you like the story? What is your favorite part? Why?
4) Show me what a happy face looks like? Show me what a sad face looks like? Can you move your face the same way I can?
5) To "cast" can mean to throw. God cares and He wants us to:

Cast all your anxiety on him because he cares for you.
1 Peter 5:7

6) Can you think of other things you would like to talk about or ask?

(Check out www.supposewithrose.com for free downloadable coloring pages or activities.)

God Is Always Chasing After You

Eight
"Not Right"

Dear Reader,

Many people knew Kayla *loved* horses, but really, they were here second love. Dolphins came first. That love soon faded when she realized she'd have to be able to get in the water to be with them. About the age of five years old, Kayla decided she wanted to be a large-animal veterinarian and wanted to be able to take care of horses and cattle.

At six, she wanted to take horse-riding lessons and began saving money to do so. We said she could sign up for lessons at seven years old, and Mom and Dad would match her savings dollar-to-dollar. On the occasions when I'd go to a gas station and grab a drink, instead of her also choosing a drink she would ask, "Mom if I don't get a drink, may I have the money to go towards my lessons instead?"

This child was dedicated and very much a plan-ahead personality.

Kayla loved her therapeutic horse-riding lessons with Mrs. Judy and her team at Equessense Therapeutic Horse Riding in Marion, Texas. Following lessons and while she was learning more about horses, another dream rose in Kayla's heart: "I want to be pulled by a horse in a carriage." We'd always joke that she should have been born in the pioneer days.

Her Paw-Paw (Great Grandpa) heard her dream and he found a way to make it happen. I tell you this child felt like she was in the clouds when Puff pulled her around. Puff was this little runt of a horse and couldn't have weighed more than 350 lbs. She even made up his own little theme song with the tune of "Puff, the Magic Dragon." They were quite the pair. Still, to this day, some of us believe he's a miniature horse, while others would title him a Shetland pony. He looked like a little puff of cotton in the winter. So fluffy. But Puff had a problem. Puff would not turn correctly.

"Mom, Puff listens to me on all of my directions. He listens if I want him to speed up, if I want him to stop, or if I ask him to back up or turn to the right. He listens to all those ways but not left. Puff will not turn to the left. What do I do?" Kayla truly was perplexed as to how to get this pony to go the "right" way.

After a series of attempts, such as training more, getting him to where left was his only option, walking him in circles to the left, etc., she finally placed a blindfold across his eyes. Guess what happened then. The stubborn little creature had no choice but to listen to the directions Kayla gave him. At first, the blindfold Kayla used was two bandanas. Imagine this little white ball of fluff with a red and blue bandana pulling a pony-sized black carriage on the bank of a square-shaped pond, not much more than six feet wide on the banks, turning right at every single right and then getting turned around to turn left at every single left. Kayla felt quite accomplished to have figured out how to train him to be compliant to her directions.

While we were in the hospital, Kayla knew she'd struggle to be able to see all that was coming her way. All the medical diagnosis and tests were overwhelming. She had an ability to understand things in a way that exceeded her years, so she reflected on Puff and the bandana.

"Mom, I don't want to know stuff so long before we are going through it, especially if it is just going to change. May I wear a bandana like Puff?"

"Yes, you may."

"But Mom, do you promise to tell me what I need to know when the time is right?"

"Yes Darling. I will tell you what you need to know is happening when the time is right," I promised.

Scripture:

"I have much more to say to you, more than you can now bear.
John 16:12

He has made everything beautiful in its time. He has also set eternity in the human heart; yet no one can fathom what God has done from beginning to end.
Ecclesiastes 3:11

LOVE Affirmed:

It is okay to not know what is to come. Scripture tells us no one can fathom, or understand, what God has done from beginning to end. Yet we are wired to want to know. We are veiled for our own protection that we can bear whatever comes when it the time is right, and we must trust the Holy Spirit will tell us and guide us when it is time. Like wet clay with mere lumpy form being worked into an artful pitcher or vase, these pieces of Scripture took form for Kayla and me. We spoke about how Jesus told the disciples they could not bear to know all that was to come, but a Helper would join when it was time to guide them through their experiences.

The Helper, the Holy Spirit, was present. It was as though the clay pitchers were our hearts to be filled with the living water and poured out for one another and for those around us and being filled up by the love and prayers of so many.

I must offer caution here. Readers, whether you're the caregiver, or the one needing the care, don't let not your pitcher run dry by pouring out and not receiving. Find something, some way, to connect with and catch the living water God alone provides during the journey. Facing situations such as these in our own power is entirely too daunting.

In our situation, the chaplain, Child Life and Care team, and our family at church and on the home front filled this need for Kayla and I of course poured into Kayla too. These caring hearts and loving people were there for me too. However, when the pain became greatest, I withdrew. I wanted to refrain from pouring out, as all I had to pour was sorrow. I felt my pouring would have negatively hurt the people around me. And I withdrew where very few could pour into me. This affected my health, leaving me with little to nothing to pour for a time. Thankfully, God had gone before us and had placed people who would stand in the middle of all that is "me" and shake awakening to what is raw and real. Essentially, they love me enough to tell me the truth and help me despite myself.

After the loss of my mom and Kayla, I felt conviction from the Lord. Conviction from a Christian stand point happens when Gods word moves in your heart to turn from something that isn't God's best will for your life. These words came so clearly it was as if I heard Him say "Careful child, don't let your grief become bigger than me."

Please don't misunderstand. Grieving and grief is natural. It is not a sin to grieve the loss of one you love or to grieve an unmet expectation for one's life. This conviction was more like a warning from my Heavenly Father telling me, "Remember, I Am. I planned for this. I know you're sad but don't forget I'm bigger than your sadness."

Prayer:

Lord, my human nature wants to know who, what, when, where, why, and how. We are even trained in school to find answers to these questions in texts we read. Yet, that is the world. Father, let the trust that is fleeting to the flesh come to life in the person reading this, so one moment at a time, this person can bear with what You reveal. I pray the reader sees what freedom and peace there is to see and grows to trust and in Your guidance. Lord, thank You for the provision and lesson to walk by faith not by sight for Kayla through the itty-bitty horse that would not turn right and thank You that You are I Am.

Smiles to Share – Section 8

Animal Names

I love animals. I know it's hard to believe, but it's true.
Since I was young, I've loved animals, more than average kids do!
I've named some kind of silly. In a big way because it is fun.
It's often because of something the animal has done.

Like Squirrel's not a squirrel, but a chicken,
who lays an egg for me each day.
She's brown and black, small, hyper,
and bounces around in a squirrelly way.

Then there's a bull I called Rooster,
I raised him from when he was very small.
But when the sun came up every morning
I didn't hear a crow but a bawl!

I've taken care of:
a duck called Quackers, a pig named Hammy,
Pepper the heifer, a fawn named Bambi,
a turtle named Ted, Lolly, my grandma's dog,
Pumpkin, my Mimi's cat, and Jumpy the frog.
My favorite of them all is a pony.
He's white, and I braid his mane.
He pulls me behind him in a carriage.
Puff the Magic Pony is his name!

Sometimes Puff is stubborn.
He only wants to turn to the right.
But if I put on his blinders,
he must rely on me for his sight.

So many animals taught me
many useful things.
But I learned from Puff
it's better to trust directions my leader brings.

Have I told you that I love animals?
If I haven't you should know it's true!
And I want you to know it's been my pleasure,
to share some animal names with you!

Connecting Ideas:
1)   Do you have any animal stories? Pretend or real are fun to talk about.
2)   If you had a white pony, what are some names you might give it?
3)   Do you like the story? What is your favorite part? Why?
4)   What is something you always wanted to do? Have you gotten to do it?
5)   In this story, we hear about the word "trust." Sometimes we have to listen to others in what we cannot know. Jesus told his disciples

"I have much more to say to you, more than you can now bear.
John 16:12

6)   Can you think of anything else you want to talk about or ask?

(Check out www.supposewithrose.com for free downloadable coloring pages or activities.)

71

God Is Always Chasing After You

Nine
Gentle Gestures

Dear Reader,

The mood in the room seems cold after diagnosis or when complications arise. Perhaps the numbness from the shock does this. In our situation, the staff did not usually cause the cold atmosphere. "Your child has cancer," doesn't scream sunshine and roses and the medical team must relay facts, but our care team was amazing. It's just the mood that overtakes the situation.

Cold. Shock. Numb. Total overwhelm. This was indeed the case for Kayla, initially, and in a sense for Dustin following diagnosis. (For me, this came after her passing.) In our situation, the fast thinking of a thoughtful little sister provided a helpful tool, an interesting icebreaker, and reminded us of the power of a gentle gesture.

When Kayla's cancer diagnosis was confirmed in June of 2021, I returned home and called a family meeting. I had to carry the news home to my family that not only would Kayla and I not be home, but she had Acute Myeloid Leukemia, as well as an infection severely complicating our situation since she had no immune system to fight it. As you can imagine this news was heavy and felt cold. The words felt stuck in my mouth like a tongue stuck on an ice cube.

After the news was out, and so that the adults could ask frank questions, I told Haley and Madi I needed their help in gathering a list of toy animals Kayla wanted in her hospital room. Kayla had listed the names of each toy, and I knew very few of her plastic animals names. But Haley knew each of them, so she and Madi gathered the toys without hesitation. They would do anything to help.

Haley also added something Kayla had not requested: B.B., Kayla's stuffed chicken. YaYa Liz, had given this stuffed chicken to Kayla when she had learned to prevent infection, Kayla could no longer work her chickens in April of 2021. Such a thoughtful gift.

Haley and Madi walked in the room. "Momma, do you think it would be okay if B.B. goes? You know how much Kayla loves her chickens." I thought it was a wonderful addition to the list.

When Kayla saw B.B., she was quite excited. She decided B.B. would go with her everywhere. Using rubber bands, Kayla created a nest and secured B.B. to her I.V. pole. B.B. became a mascot and an icebreaker, to be introduced to every new person Kayla met.

"I'm Kayla and this is B.B." If the person didn't bite her bait in curiosity, I would step in, "Why don't you tell them what B.B. stands for?" Kayla'd smile her coy smile, look at the person intently so she could see their reaction to the fullest and say, "B.B. stands for Blue Butt."

Silly as it was, it worked. It was as though the stuffed chicken melted the cold icy mood. B.B. helped set the stage for every new introduction, even down in surgical prep and in the waiting room when B.B. inevitably had to wait with Dustin and me.

Sometimes in life our minds just have too much to process well, and there is no harm in having a practiced response to these stressful situations. It varies, given the place you are, but it is entirely okay to need it, have it, and use it.

Haley later made a bracelet for Kayla but since it was so crucial that Kayla not cut herself, Kayla decided B.B. could wear the bracelet as a necklace, and she said, "Now you can tell Haley the bracelet is always with me." Overall B.B. represented deep thoughtfulness, both in the initial gifting but also in Haley and Madi's gentle gesture. This thoughtfulness, and so many gentle gestures like it, made such a difference for Kayla's hospital stay.

Scripture:

Let your gentleness be evident to all. The Lord is near.
Philippians 4:5

After the earthquake came a fire, but the LORD was not in the fire. And after the fire came a gentle whisper.
1 Kings 19:12

LOVE Affirmed:

Gentle gestures remind us and others that the Lord is near. We are in the world marred by sin and death, and while God is at work in, through and around us, God is not the destruction for those called by Him. God is the calm in the storm not the calamity. He called Noah to build the ark. He parted the Red Sea. He made a way for us to be with Him through His Son. God is a faithful Father who is full of gentleness along the way if we seek Him.

Our hospital room was a constant reminder of gentle gestures. B.B. was just one of the many. We had cards on the wall that Kayla would walk to for exercise and encouragement. I would change them out so there was always something new. One package we received included cards and drawings from an entire classroom. Several athletes did things too—a young man placed Kayla's favorite verse on his football helmet, an entire softball team made and shared flyers, a swimmer marked her leg and back at a meet, a cheerleader wore Kayla's initials on her cheek. Texts from teachers and friends, meals for the family, and so very much more served as reminders that God was with us through the struggle.

While we had a whole village to pull from, I recognize that's not always the case. If you're in a position where you do not have a village reach out to you, I assure you there are resources available. Perhaps making a call to reach out to a church or a social worker is a good step. Also, you can find many resources online, too, but first, don't hesitate to call upon our faithful Father.

Prayer:

Father, life doesn't feel gentle in times of illness or loss. Honestly, it feels quite harsh. But help us, help the reader and me, know You're near through the work of Your faithful followers. Move on the heart of the person in the struggle to ask and accept help when the burden is great. Lord, you know our needs, our hearts, and our pains. Thank You that no matter what, love remains.

Smiles to Share – Section 9

Mrs. Skunk Runs Amuck

Out in the moonlight for a walk under the stars,
Mrs. Skunk went—her minding her business,
and my family minding ours.

Suddenly, right in front of us we were surprised
when we found ourselves stopped stuck staring
in two shimmery beady black eyes.

Way closer than any of us wanted to be,
freeze don't sneeze, I thought,
Mrs. Skunk's tail grew by two babies.

I wondered where their skunk daddy might be.
The darkness of the night made me question,
Should I stay here or should I flee.

We each had many choices we could choose to make,
but we each hoped for the other, no fast,
(or stinky) action would they take.

God Is Always Chasing After You

Dad whispered, "Go back, slowly, one step at a time."
While Mrs. Skunk stood still like a statue,
frozen, with her eyes watching mine.

Neither Trip the dog nor the skunk kits walked away,
so Mrs. Skunk felt she was left no choice
but to run amuck and spray.

Off ran the skunk kits fast. Off ran Mrs. Skunk.
Here came Trip prancing proudly,
and oh, I tell you, man, he stunk!

"Stay back Trip." Dad said, then we all sighed a big sigh,
when Trip stopped, turned, and moved quickly
to the fishpond nearby.

I guess Trip decided he needed a quick bath.
Because he jumped in for a swim.
Did we avoid the amuck skunk's aftermath?

"No! Stop! Trip, get back!" Dad tried to get Trip to stay.
But Trip was excited and he's playful.
He thought Dad was trying to play.

Dad stepped between us and made sure we were all hid.
That's when Trip shook off the stinky water.
I'm not kidding. Yes, he sure did.

It's morning now and wow! Do Trip and Dad's clothes stink!
But I'm left with a few little questions.
Maybe you know the secret link.

How is it the skunk, who can make such a big stink,
not stink before spraying. What do you think?
It's so bad it's hard to not blink!

We had no idea Mrs. Skunk and her kits were right there.
Wouldn't that stink get stuck in her big,
bushy, black and white tail hair?

I like to know what's coming. When I can't, that stinks.
But yesterday I learned a parent's protection is real
and love moves faster than an eye blinks.

Connecting Ideas :
1)   What smell makes you happy? Why do you like that smell?
2)   What smells make you say yuck?
3)   Do you like the story? What is your favorite part? Why?
4)   Do you think someone would protect you from a spraying skunk or would you protect someone else from one?
5)   In this story we read about a father whose gentle gestures protected the children from a stinky situation. The Bible says:

Let your gentleness be evident to all. The Lord is near.
Philippians 4:5

6)   Can you think of anything else you would like to talk about or ask?

(Check out www.supposewithrose.com for free downloadable coloring pages or activities.)

Ten
Bag to Bear

Dear Reader,

The go bag. Many have heard of these in relation to pregnancy. Basically, it's a bag ready to go with the necessities for the anticipated event as it comes on without warning. If you were to compare these bags, sure there are some similarities in their contents, but oh, so many possibilities.

In my pregnancy "go bags" I had my favorite button-up nightgown, toothbrush, toothpaste, what I wanted my baby to come home in, and extra underwear. That was all.

In Mom's hospital "go bag," I kept a bottle of each of her meds with a three-day supply, reading glasses, a deck of cards, a change of clothes, a list of phone numbers, a family picture, a note pad, and a pen.

Kayla, however, created more than one "go bag." This child had priorities and knew her mind needed to keep busy.

"Go bags" went with us to every oncology appointment, except the first and last. We were seen nearly every week from April 13 to June 28. We went to each visit with the understanding we could be sent to the ER, due to blood levels. In a way, we'd let our guard down and had taken the seriousness for granted the last day. Kayla didn't even give Grandma hugs and had not made a point to spend special sister time with Haley (and Madi, if she was at the house), which also had become routine as part of her own "what if" plan. So, when we were told we had to go to the hospital, in addition to the emotions surrounding going to the hospital and the unknown, Kayla felt an urgency to go back home for the hugs and the bags.

"Momma, please, please take me home. I need my grandma hug. What if Grandma dies before I get out? I need my sister time. Haley won't understand why I didn't come back today," she begged.

"Honey, I can't take you home. I cannot risk your getting sick. You can't fight anything off. Baby, Momma's sorry, but no."

I wanted so badly to be able to bring her home; I wanted to be able to say, "Yes."

This day they didn't allow us to stay in the ER waiting area; they sent us straight back to a room. We only had one nurse in the ER department, and she wore full protective gear. They were being extremely careful. Thankfully, Kayla had a small crocheting project with her to busy her hands.

Everything after this hit like a whirlwind. Oncology floor. Blood tests. Strict rules. Bed sheet changes. HCG wipes. Unfamiliar terms. Lots of people. Lots of information. Lots of ill children.

Once we were settled into our room, Dustin—Daddy—brought us our bags. I allowed Kayla to only have one in the room at a time at first, the bag with her animal book. The rest took up residence in Silver the Minivan. This arrangement gave me an excuse to take a walk from time to time.

Now this "book" really is a three-inch binder overflowing with page sleeves, each holding pictures of animals she had cared for and a description of the animal. She started the book in fourth grade with a picture album and animal log specifically of the chicks her third-grade classroom had given her. In fifth grade, the book took off as her science teacher challenged her to also translate the book into Spanish to share with the class. She was in a dual language program.

Utilizing this book I speak of, Kayla did her own husbandry experiments with her chickens. She truly never had a dull moment. She found something to learn at each phase and from each failure. So, when Kayla was sitting in her hospital bed and working on this monstrosity, she had the perfect opportunity to talk about all those animals. It became a point of interest for the staff. She even had a key on the pages: S- sold, D- died, B- butchered. The facts of farm life were news for non-farm people.

Attentive as the nurses were, they commonly asked, "Kayla, what's in that bag." Most of the time, they were surprised at the things she would pull out.

One bag had crocheting items. She made rally caps for herself, Grandma, Aunt Amber, Madi, and me. Then she heard it was one of the custodial staff's daughter's first birthday, and she paused in crocheting her rally cap to create a birthday gift. Another bag had art supplies and books for reading. Besides her clothing bag, she also had her guitar case, complete with notes.

The time came when the physical bags no longer mattered. What did matter, however, was the bag of her experiences, support, faith, and love.

Scripture:

As Jesus and his disciples were on their way, he came to a village where a woman named Martha opened her home to him. She had a sister called Mary, who sat at the Lord's feet listening to what her said. But Martha was distracted by all the preparations that had to be made. She came to him and asked, "Lord, don't you care that my sister has left me to do the work by myself? Tell her to help me!" "Martha, Martha," the Lord answered, "you are worried and upset about many things, but few things are needed—or indeed only one. Mary has chosen what is better, and it will not be taken away from her."

Luke 10: 38–42

As the Father has loved me, so have I loved you. Now remain in my love. If you keep my commands, you will remain in my love, just as I have kept my Father's commands and remain in his love. I have told you this so that my joy may be in you and that your joy may be complete. My command is this: Love each other as I have loved you.

John 15:9–12

LOVE Affirmed:

We think we need many things in this world. Really, we need only to sit at the feet of Jesus and seek the truth to help cast out fear. I know in these ailing times, times of taking care of a loved one, or the business part that follows loss, sitting at the feet of our Lord seems counterproductive. The fact is, in the end, our relationship with the Lord through our faith is the thing that can align priorities, bring comfort, and calm worries and anxieties.

The one bag stayed with us and moved with us everywhere, even if the physical bags did not: Our faith bag. A Bible, a devotional, and her crosses were in the physical bag. Daily, we read a devotional and kept the Bible on hand. When Kayla could not speak due to the breathing tube, she wanted to hear the devotional, and would request that her "Jesus music" be played. Ultimately, her faith bag was the only "go bag" needed.

One memory I will forever cherish happened just two days before her passing. It turned out to be the last night Kayla was outwardly responsive. We had her faith music playing, and I was at my perch, bedside, holding her hand. She started "singing" with the music. For four songs, she moved her lips along and we "sang." We worshipped God together. The last songs we worshipped together were:

"Is He Worthy," by Chris Tomlin
"God Only Knows," by For King and Country
"More Than Anything," by Natalie Grant
"Jireh," by Elevation Worship.

In Kayla's faith bag was an intimate relationship with the Lord that allowed her to sing silently with a resounding voice. A voice that still echo's in the minds of all those who knew her. What a gift it was from God to know my daughter knew, the Truth. She knew Jesus made eternity available to us because of God's love. She yearned for His presence rather than His blessings. What a gift Kayla knew no matter what the name of Jesus is enough. And our Messiah holds forever those He loves.

Prayer:
God, You're enough, indeed. You can take all we have and all we are grieving. We must grieve what doesn't fulfill our expectations. Inherently, we look to receive health; inherently, we look to receive good things; inherently we expect a loving God to remove hard and heavy bags in this world. Indeed, You do remove them eventually. But Father, we often must let them go and gain contentment in our relationship with You to ultimately trust *everything* to You, including the person we love and ourselves—even when we blame You, God. Give us the wherewithal to pick up the faith bag. Let it be our ultimate "go bag" in every stage of our journey to be like Jesus.

Smiles to Share – Section 10

Ready Beaver

"TIMBER!" Buddy Beaver called out loud. Then he started singing as the tree fell down, down, down to the ground.

"Why are you singing, B.B?" I asked.

"Because I want everyone I know I am H-A-P-P-Y, happy, Tiny."

I did not understand why he was happy to move away, "But you won't have me to hang out with, and we won't get to play."

"I know change is hard, Tiny, and I will miss you. It's just time for Ruby and me to see what love can do."

"What if I went with you? I could help you."

"No, Tiny, it's not the right time now but you'll know.."

Dad Beaver's tail clapped the water, calling in his kits. We dove in to join—Mom, Dad, Ruby, Jess, and Fritz.

The plants were stacked high for a feast. And all the family sat together in their seats.

"Today is special," said Dad, "B.B. and Ruby are ready beavers, tried and true. Sure they'll have troubles but all ready beavers do."

"Just try your best in all you do. Love God first. Love others, too. Know you are prayed for. Know you are loved. Know you are a blessing from God up above."

My sister Ruby was smiling, but I could see fear in her eyes. Mom's reassurance was no surprise.

"You are ready. The time is right. You'll soon have your own lodge to care for day and night." Mom said, "Jesus told us troubles will come but take heart I have overcome the world."

With that B.B. and Ruby dropped in, and the water swirled.

I jumped in, too. I wasn't ready to let Buddy Beaver go.

Dad jumped in beside me. He said, "Let's go for a quick swim." He asked B.B. and Ruby to wait for him.

"Change is hard, Tiny. I remember when we let our oldest kits go. Your Mom said yes, but I said no. I met a wise owl after I stepped away; she asked me a question I remember to this day."

"Who, who, who, are you thinking of?" That's what Owlie said. "I tell you Tiny the biggest sadness went through my head. Think about it son, take a moment to pray. Then we need to get back to say 'see you later' before they go away."

Dad had a point. He helped me see, "I don't like that I was thinking if me."

Dad whispered, "Loving others makes H-A-P-P-Y, happy, happen in the heart."

We did a big Beaver family hug after we returned. I hope I never forget the lesson I learned.

Together Mom, Dad, and us little beavers said the mantra again; together we waved 'see you later,' as the ready beavers set out for their swim.

"Try your best in all you do. Love God first. Love others too. Know you are prayed for. Know you are loved. Know you are a blessing from God up above."

Connecting Ideas:
1)   Can you think of any other animals that swim? Which is your favorite?
2)   What is something Mom or Dad always says?
3)   If you were going to build your own house, what would it have in it? How would it look?
4)   How are you a blessing to someone?
5)   Joy is a different word for happy. Joy is made complete through love. The Bible says:

> *I [Jesus] have told you this so that my joy may be in you and that your joy may be complete. My command is this: Love each other as I have loved you.*
> **John 15: 11-12**

6)   Can you think of anything else you want to talk about or ask?

(Check out www.supposewithrose.com for free downloadable coloring pages or activities.)

Eleven
Smiles to Share

Dear Reader,

We were in the ICU. Kayla's breathing and overall health wasn't in a good place, and we were bordering on more invasive breathing support than her already-high-flow oxygen. On this particular day, our church family had organized a blood drive in honor of Kayla. We received many updates as sleeves were rolled or as prayers went up.

Kayla's countenance perked. The event going on helped her feel as though she wasn't taking as much, knowing so many would give freely of themselves. Seventy-one units were collected that day in her honor and more later from repeat donors or those who couldn't make it to the truck on the day of the event. On the tails of others giving of themselves, Kayla asked if she could draw a picture that "might help others smile" on the glass door of the room. I cautioned, "They may have to erase it, but I am sure they won't mind."

While she drew, the hospital staff took notice. Happily, she exclaimed, "Hey Mom it's making the nurses smile, too. I'm glad."

If you look at the cover of this book you will see my illustrator Dave's depiction of a real photograph. Who knew a blue horse and butterfly would become my farmgirl's last statement for others in this world. For those that knew her, the image was all too fitting.

Kayla wasn't one for cartoony animal figures and had she a choice, that horse would not have been blue.

"Mom, blue is not a real horse color," she said jokingly in a matter of fact tone.

With her drawing finished, Kayla was exhausted. Like a sponge wrung dry, she squeezed every drop of energy and love she had into that picture from her golden heart. We settled her into bed, and she was placed on the bi-pap machine. I read a list of various Scriptures aloud and through headshakes, a head tilt, a single nod, or a double thumbs up, Kayla selected the ones she felt belonged. The double thumbs up verse was Isaiah 58:11. The head tilt verse was 1 John 4:19.

Scripture:

The Lord will guide you continually, giving you water when you are dry and restoring your strength. You will be like a well-watered garden, like an ever-flowing spring.

Isaiah 58:11

We love Him because He [God] first loved us.

1 John 4:19

Jesus Christ is the same yesterday and today and forever.

Hebrews 13:8

Kayla chose to consider people around her. Empathetically, she remembered every one of the people there and the fact their families were going through something hard.

"People aren't in ICU because they want to be," she explained to one of the nurses, "unless, like you, they're called to be," she corrected herself, "even then it has to be hard."

The nurse looked curiously at Kayla, trying to understand her comment about it being hard. Kayla paused to catch her breath between words, "It has to be hard to see all the pain and suffering. God may work through your hands, heart, and knowledge, and you maybe good, but you can't fix everything."

This child's wisdom and compassion far exceeded her years. The nurse left the room shortly after that—to gather himself and his emotions, I am sure.

This gesture from Kayla came in the midst of her lungs, kidneys, and liver failing, and her body falling septic, poisoned by its own illness. The gesture served not only as a reminder we have smiles to share but a reminder and an understanding that God is the restorer of strength and health. He, and He alone, has the ability to continually guide us through our lives, struggles and all. Readers, let not your hearts be deceived or burdened carrying or casting fault for your loved one's (or your patients) ailment or pain. Illness, brokenness, death is a reflection and a result of a fallen world.

LOVE Affirmed:

Thinking of or considering others through Christ unleashes great power, Holy Spirit power. If by chance you don't know what I mean by this I encourage you to seek out spiritual counsel. The Holy Spirit is who Jesus left behind as our helper in the world. Jesus said to love others as we love ourselves. Through this experience, I can honestly say I believe He left these instructions just as much for those doing the loving as for those being loved.

One emotional battle that surfaces often is the idea Kayla "missed out" in life. Sure, she never experienced many things in this world we'd typically consider to be part of a full life. Or, rather, she missed the life I'd mapped out in my mind for her. Yet, when I work through those thoughts and rest in the Holy Spirit, when I let Him guide me, as Kayla's selected verse reminded, I recognize she did experience the life God allowed and now experiences so very much more.

Remember, little things go a long way. The desire of Kayla's heart was to make others smile. For all those last days, when Kayla could not speak, she could watch and see the passersby smile. Those smiles were as bright to her as the bright morning star guiding the shepherds to their Savior Jesus. The smiles were a gift from the Lord for Kayla—blessings, answered prayers, restoration of strength—so she could be like an ever-flowing spring, just as the verse claimed, to endure the journey before her. Reader, let not your hearts be deceived or burdened carrying or casting fault for ailment or pain. Illness, brokenness, death is a reflection and a result of a fallen world.

Prayer:

Father, I pray this memory made someone smile today. At the same time, Father, every journey differs. Helping others indeed releases Your power. So does gratitude and receiving a blessing of help from others. You're the One who lifts our hearts and lifts our heads. You're the One who offers extreme grace, forgiveness, patience, and strength to persevere. I ask every reader to hear your voice whispering, "Where you are I Am."

God is love. God, You are bigger than everything we are facing. The journey is hard and sometimes our emotions toward You are harsh. But You're the very One who provided us with emotions. You loved first. Thank You. Your love does not depend upon temporary emotions, but upon Your redeeming love and salvation through Jesus as our Savior. Thank you for every smile shared then and now. Until the day you call us home to You, Father, I chose You to guide me.

Blue Horse and Butterfly

Blue the horse said to the caterpillar Cruz one day,
"Let's spend time together, what do you say?"
Cruz really didn't know what they'd do,
but said, "Sure, I'll spend time with you."
Their play continued day after day I heard.
Cruz grew encouraged by Blues every word.
"I'm sorry," said Cruz, "I'm really feeling tired."
Blue explained no apology was required.
Cruz decided he'd nap for a while.
"I will protect you," Blue said with a peaceful smile.
Blue knew Cruz had come to an important time.
One prepared for Cruz by his maker Divine.
Blue prayed for his friend, "God may he come to know your love for him.
May Cruz shine for You Lord not flutter through life tossed by a whim."
Upon waking Cruz shouted, "Blue look what I did. I'm a butterfly."
Before Blue knew it, Cruz along with his ego took flight in the sky.
After some time, Blue, being the praying friend he was
chased after Cruz and reminded him God transformed him in love.
"God gave you this gift of beauty and flight.
Singing praise to Him, not bragging, would be what is right."
Stubbornly Cruz filled his time with pride and sin.
"I deserve it," said Cruz, "You say God did something. I ask when?"
Blue stayed faithful, prayed even more, sometimes he cried.
Never losing hope someday his friend would be in Heaven by his side.

God Is Always Chasing After You

Then it happened, oh glorious day! Cruz flew to Blue,
he looked down. "Why do you care about what I do?
You've been a good friend to me, but I haven't to you."
Blue said, "I belong to I Am, like mine His love for you is true.
Nothing can keep Him. Love will not stop chasing after you."
Blue had given Cruz grace, love he did not deserve.
Cruz drooped his head and lost his nerve.
"It's not a matter of what is worked for or earned by you,
It is all about what God called His only Son Jesus to do.
He gave His life to cover our sin.
To be forgiven, believing in Jesus is where you begin."
Cruz brightened, almost as if to glow.
He turned a great circle and said, "Really! Is that so?"
"Surely it is," Blue joined in the praise.
There the two were celebrating with flutters and neighs.
All around the pair others had been watching a while,
Even those that were troubled or in pain could not help but smile.

This story was inspired by a picture a girl named Kayla drew.
She loved others and she wanted you to know
God's Love is Chasing After You.
"Friend, stop running!" She'd say, "Turn to God your face.
Let Love Himself hug You. He is with you in this place."

Connecting Ideas:
1)   Can you move like a caterpillar? How about a butterfly? And now a horse?
2)   If you wrote the story would you have used a butterfly or something else? Why?
3)   What is your favorite kind of bug? Why?
4)   Do you have a good friend who prays for you?
5)   Caterpillars change into butterflies. You and I change too. But do you know who doesn't? The Bible tells us:

Jesus Christ is the same yesterday and today and forever.
Hebrews 13:8

6)   Can you think of anything else you want to talk about or ask?

(Check out www.supposewithrose.com for free downloadable coloring pages or activities.)

God Is Always Chasing After You

Twelve
Water Wounds

Dear Reader,
The nurses and staff were a godsend during those long nights in the ICU.

"Kayla will tell you if it is time, Momma. You'll know," several seasoned ICU Nurses reassured me, as I began wondering if I was pressing on for Kayla's improvement or for myself. One nurse shared an experience from her medical mission trip to Africa. She shared that the mothers tending their ill children praised God for the time they had together even as they waited knowing death was near for them. I would ponder all of the comments in prayer.

"Water," Kayla's eyes would meet mine, and she would simply mouth the word, "water" repeatedly. The simplest ask on the face of this Earth, and I had to deny her request. This was one of the hardest parts of the experience. The Word tells us to "give drink to our enemies" after all, and I couldn't "give drink" to my own daughter. I'd reflect on all the animals she tended, and the thing that mattered the absolute most was if the animals had water. This will forever hit deep as I can imagine this was among her thoughts too.

These "water wounds," as I call them, cut a canyon straight through my heart. Denying the wants of any ailing person hurts those who love and are caring for them. I would pray for His guidance, as the temptation to put extra water on her mouth swab was great. The Holy Spirit would bring John 19:30 to mind every time.

"If You are trying to help me understand the feeling You had of watching Your Son, I get it. Please heal my baby." Then later the question, "Are You preparing me? Is this why You keep bringing this scripture to my mind?" Immediately after Jesus' thirst was answered, He gave up His Spirit.

"No!"

Jumbled thoughts bolted through my head and ripped at my heart. Words so mixed up even my own mind had no clue what it was thinking or praying.

"Oh Father? Help me." I wept so and do still as I go back to those moments.

Following this, I became more intentional talking to Kayla about knowing how hard she's trying, how proud I was of her, no matter what, and she'd never disappoint us. When she fought sleep for fear of not waking, I would reassure her.

"Don't be afraid, Baby; like you said, if God calls you home, it's not goodbye, it's see you later."

I began reading her jokes too. Her favorite was about a cow:

Studies show cows produce more milk when farmers talk to them.
It was a case of in one ear out the udder.

She and I would converse about how much milk her cow, Pepper, produced and that the joke was about her and Pepper, she'd smile every time.

In short, I "coached" less to her about fighting and tried to be more "in the moment" with her. All the while, hoping I was hearing the Lord wrong.

Scripture:

Later, knowing that everything had now been finished, and so that Scripture would be fulfilled, Jesus said, "I am thirsty." A jar of wine vinegar was there, so they soaked a sponge in it, put the sponge on a stalk of the hyssop plant, and lifted it to Jesus' lips. When he had received the drink, Jesus said, "It is finished." With that, he bowed his head and gave up his spirit.

John 19:28–30

Be on your guard; stand firm in the faith; be courageous; be strong.
Do everything in love.

1 Corinthians 16:13–14

LOVE Affirmed:

Sometimes deep thought is helpful, other times it's downright painful, most of the time it's both; and in this pondering of thoughts, we can lose opportunities of today. Just as Jesus prepared His disciples, the Holy Spirit was and is preparing us. Many prayer warriors have since shared a shift in their prompting as well.

On October 27, 2021 Kayla was given approval for ice chips. My heart sunk. I tried to rejoice with her for her orange popsicle. But this clearance was like the confirmation to me that I was going to bury my baby. This approval prompted my making arrangements for Haley to come that day, no time to waste. Haley needed her "I love you, Sister." moments, and we needed Haley to be able to ask the hard questions. I flashed to the two as babies when at about 6 weeks old Haley "fell in love" with her sister

The sisters shared a beautiful moment. Each missed walking and talking together. Haley told Kayla she was the best big sister ever. Kayla had listed a few other things she wanted to say prior to Haley getting there. I read the words as Kayla looked into Haley's hazel eyes. In the moment it was so beautiful yet at the same time excruciating.

Exhausted, Kayla fell asleep. While she napped, Haley drew a picture on the glass window too. Hers was a destination with a fruit tree, blue clouds, and clear skies—and the pink butterfly was now blue and the horse was not there. When I asked her many weeks later what her picture meant, she said God was inside the butterfly and guiding it to Heaven.

On the drive home after the visit Haley asked if Kayla was going to die. I explained Kayla was very sick and the test results were worse. I told Haley that Kayla would need help breathing for the rest of her life and most likely wouldn't be able to come home for a long time, if at all, due to the level of her need. I reminded Haley that ultimately God knows and has a plan.

"Mom don't be mad." She paused for my reassurance. "I think it would be better for Kayla to be with God . . . " Like thunderclaps in a storm, sobs shook her body between her words.

"I'm not mad. Please finish what you want to say, Sweetheart."

"I want her here. But I love her, and I know we'll be together in Heaven. No animals, not able to talk. Hurting so bad. That's just not for Kay-Kay!"

Enter the prayer pause.

Lord help my words. Father help me contain my emotion that she may see You and my sincerity. Lord how is it this child is only ten.

"Sweet Sister, there is nothing wrong with you loving your sister enough to want her to be happy and out of pain. There is nothing wrong with trusting God's Word enough to know Heaven is waiting. That is selfless love." I reached my arm over to her and hugged her with my tears rolling. "It's loving her first, Baby. It is beautiful."

Prayer:
Lord Jesus, thank You that many years ago You denied the drink first on the cross. You fully experienced the crucifixion. You prayed to the Father in Your agony.

You asked the forgiveness for those who persecuted You.

"Forgive them Father they know not what they do."

You took drink then called out, "It is finished."

Because of Your choice of obedience, because of Your love for each of us, we can look forward to a reunion in Heaven. I ask Your healing be awaited with full confidence, may there be no fear in the everlasting. I ask every ounce of sadness, pain, and fear be something each Reader knows You hold in the palm of Your hand. The same hand Father that resurrected Jesus.

Smiles to Share – Section 12

Upside-down Singing Possum

Awake one night, I heard some chirping.
I wondered to myself, what could it be?
I thought it could be baby birds calling,
From a nest, outside my window, in the tree.

I shook my head and said, "Maybe,
but this doesn't sound like a bird I'd ever heard."
I imagined a creepy creature singing.
In the still of night, like at camp, without music or words.

The more I thought about it,
The more unsettled and fearful I became,
So finally, I got brave, honest, and open-minded,
I made knowing what the sound was my aim.

I walked to my window very slowly.
I didn't interrupt the jazzy interesting song.
It sure wasn't birdies that were lonely,
turned out I was totally wrong.

God Is Always Chasing After You

Hanging by tails, eyes gleaming like gems,
Was an entire possum family.
Some say they're pests, but I watched them.
It was like they became pets for me.

A family of upside-down, singing possums,
Hung outside my window from a tree!
I don't mind saying it was pretty awesome
to watch them grow and hear them sing!

Possums, like me, can be awfully misunderstood.
Think about it, maybe you'll agree it's awesome.
Even if yours doesn't sing as good,
to meet a family of upside-down, singing possums.

Not knowing had me unsettled and blinded.
I wonder if some fears are sometimes just things misunderstood.
If I let myself be brave, honest, and open-minded,
Perhaps things I think are bad can also be good?

Connecting Ideas:
1) Have you ever seen a possum? How would you describe them?
2) Tell me about a song you know. Can we sing it together?
3) Do you like the story? What is your favorite part? Why?
4) Do you know what it means to be misunderstood? Or can you tell me a time you felt you have to be brave?
5) In this story, we hear the word "brave." Another word for brave is "courageous." It means to do something even when you are afraid. The Bible says:

Be on your guard; stand firm in the faith; be courageous; be strong. Do everything in love.
1 Corinthians 16:13–14

6) Can you think of anything else you want to talk about or ask?

(Check out www.supposewithrose.com for free downloadable coloring pages or activities.)

Thirteen
Let Live

Dear Reader,

A saying in this world is, "Live and let live." Typically, this saying refers to living in peace with one another, not passing judgment on them, or really, placing your beliefs onto them.

But in our case, this saying hits differently. Don't get me wrong, a person has a right to choose how he or she lives and that opportunity to choose goes both ways. But choice includes the consequences that follow. By far the hardest choice next to living for Christ in our lives was the choice to let Kayla live. We had to choose to love Kayla and trust God.

In a last-ditch effort, the physicians decided to throw all that could be done down in the field to improve Kayla's failing lungs. Even with 100 percent oxygen support, her oxygen saturation levels were declining well below acceptable ranges dipping into the 70's. She was not a candidate for lung transplant because her cancer diagnosis was too recent. And our "sitting in our discomfort" was no longer showing benefit.

Friday October 29 into Saturday October 30, it was evident we were not having the desired outcome. Her numbers were not improving even in the tiniest ways.

I was relieved Saturday as Dustin arrived; I had not even stepped away to pick up my phone. Her heart rate and saturation numbers dropped if I wasn't in physical contact with her somehow. I was stroking her last strands of hair and her eyebrows, as he walked in the room. We had the conversation no parents should ever have to have.

We didn't need to hear the words. When the doctor entered the room, we knew. If I am honest, the only real part of that conversation I recall clearly was the question, "Is there a day you want to avoid?"

The question felt backhanded in the moment. It was the affirmation, as many nurses had advised us, that Kayla was letting us know. I swallowed hard to choke back all the words that rushed to my mind.

What kind of question is that? How dare he assume we would want our child suffering extra. Of course, there are days we want to avoid this decision—try today, tomorrow, and every day following. That's my baby; I don't want her to hurt. Doesn't this guy know it is with God's power alone that we will live. Of course, we want to let her live. He is just doing his job. How in the world would you ask someone this question? God, please? Say this isn't happening.

I could only shake my head, "No."

"Today then?" He clarified. Many sentiments followed before the doctor left the room.

Nurses came in and out and had many questions, including if we wanted to call anyone to come. We opted not. Invites had been extended previously to this day and Kayla had been resistant to facetiming on her worst days. She did not want anyone who did not have to see her so ill to see her. In a way it was a way she was protecting others. Instead of calling friends or family to make their way to the hospital, we asked that they invite the hospital family, if they felt led, to join us.

Scripture:

He will wipe every tear from their eyes. There will be no more death' or mourning or crying or pain, for the old order of things has passed away.
Revelation 21:4

Listen, I tell you a mystery: we will not all sleep, but we will all be changed-- in a flash, in the twinkling of an eye, at the last trumpet. For the trumpet will sound, the dead will be raised imperishable, and we will be changed.
1 Corinthians 15:51–52

I have told you these things, so that in me [Jesus] you may have peace. In this world you will have trouble. But take heart! I have overcome the world.

LOVE Affirmed:

Only the Triune God, the Father, Son, and Holy Spirit, can turn the most painful journeys possible to experience into beautiful and meaningful moments. I believe this is truly the case for Kayla's dying moments.

It was Saturday. Typically, the weekends at the hospital were days fewer services were readily available. Not this Saturday. The staff of the hospital began to line the hall, including many who were not scheduled for the day. A different physician than the one we initially spoke with came in the room and explained he had to verify what we were doing.

Somehow the words choked out of my mouth, "It seems God is calling her today. We need to let my baby rest in peace." The doctor looked at Dustin, and a head nod confirmed what words couldn't.

The room filled with love. People who'd poured themselves into our family throughout this journey with Kayla and her fight filed in. One nurse, Anne, who seemed to carry a special draw to Kayla, approached and asked if she could talk to Kayla as she left, if my words failed. We had no objection.

Dustin and I shared our love and final words with our baby girl. We told her how blessed we were to be a part of her life and how we were so proud to call her ours that she will forever be one of the best gifts God ever gave us. We told her, "We will hurt big, but love will get us through."

Then, as I had promised and because it was time, I told Kayla what was about to happen.

"Okay Kayla, God decided He wants to heal you in His presence. The doctors are going to turn the machine breathing for you down, and then turn the machine off. Your eyes will be closing in death here, but when you open them you will be in the presence of Jesus, no more pain or tears, Darling. We love you too much to keep you here. We will see you when we get there."

I tried to sing the song "Precious Lord Take my Hand," but the words faded as I heard Anne quoting God's promises in my baby's ear.

A single tear fell from Kayla's eye, and I wiped it away. I believe she heard me. Her tears were no more, and a peaceful resting look overcame her face as I felt her heart beat its last.

In the midst of the most painful time, this death of my daughter's body was indeed the most beautiful way possible I could imagine seeing her go. Like a leaf falling gracefully to the ground, it was as though God's hands cradled her into His presence. In a way, it felt like I was passing my baby over to my Heavenly Father, and He was saying, "It's time child; live and let her live."

Prayer:
Precious Heavenly Father, I know this isn't the story many in their final moments on this side of Your Glory experience. But all too often, we hear the other stories or see them played out. May this sharing offer a sense of comfort in what hope can do. May those reading or hearing this know if they are facing death of their physical bodies as Your word says in 1 Corinthians 15: 51–52, in the twinkling of an eye the dead will be raised imperishable! Not because of who they are or what they have done but because of Your Love through your Son Jesus.

May all those reading this be encouraged by 1 Thessalonians 4:13–18.

Brothers and sisters, we do not want you to be uninformed about those who sleep in death, so that you do not grieve like the rest of mankind, who have no hope. For we believe that Jesus died and rose again, and so we believe that God will bring with Jesus those who have fallen asleep in him. According to the Lord's word, we tell you that we who are still alive, who are left until the coming of the Lord, will certainly not precede those who have fallen asleep. For the Lord himself will come down from heaven, with a loud command, with the voice of the archangel and with the trumpet call of God, and the dead in Christ will rise first. After that, we who are still alive and are left will be caught up together with them in the clouds to meet the Lord in the air. And so we will be with the Lord forever.
1 Thessalonians 4:13–17

Smiles to Share – Section 13

Ladybug Landing

A ladybug landed on Amanda's shoulder one day.
Amanda did not disturb her,
So, the ladybug said she would stay.

The ladybug was special.
Calling her "ladybug" seemed a shame.
Amanda quickly decided
Betty Bug was her name.

Betty Bug stayed as Amanda played.
She stayed as Amanda did her chores.
Amanda let Betty Bug stay
Until Amanda could stay no more.

It was time to go inside.
It was nighttime you see.
Amanda took Betty Bug up to a tree.
Then she kindly asked, "Please wait for me?"

Betty Bug crawled down Amanda's arm to her hand.
Then the ladybug stepped one, two, three, four, five, six tiny legs
on the tree branch to stand.
Betty Bug gazed into Amanda's light brown eyes,
"Today I will stay," was Betty Bug's silent reply.

109

Amanda told her parents of her ladybug friend.
How she asked Betty Bug to wait till she came back again.
Mom smiled at Dad, then Dad said with a grin,
"The ladybug will not be there when you go back again."

Amanda did not believe them.
She dreamed of Betty Bug that night.
She woke up hoping she was right.

At breakfast, Amanda told them, "You just wait to see.
Betty Bug, the ladybug,
Will be at the tree!"

Amanda hurried to make her bed.
She scurried for her shoes.
Amanda had thought of so much
She and Betty Bug could do.

Amanda took her parents by the arm to the tree.
She knew Betty Bug would be waiting,
They just had to see!

"Betty Bug!" she called, but Amanda could not find her.
She looked high and low.
"Betty Bug?" Amanda wondered,
Where would Betty Bug go?

Mom and Dad hugged Amanda—she was sad.
They knew she enjoyed the time they'd had.
Dad and Mom patted her tears away
When suddenly Betty Bug returned—she'd decided she would stay!

Seven nights Amanda took Betty Bug to the tree.
Each night Amanda asked her, "Betty Bug, please wait for me?"
Six nights Betty Bug crawled down Amanda's arm to her hand.
Betty Bug stepped one, two, three, four, five, six tiny little legs

God Is Always Chasing After You

On the tree to stand.

The last night, Betty Bug crawled down to Amanda's hand.
She stepped one, two, three, four, five, six little legs,
But on the tree, she would not stand.

Amanda knew it was Betty Bug's turn—she had to go away.
A tear rolled down Amanda's cheek as she lifted her arm to say,
"Betty Bug, my ladybug, I am thankful for your stay."
"Betty Bug, my ladybug, now fly away!"

Connecting Ideas:
1) What is the best breakfast?
2) What is your favorite insect or your least favorite insect?
3) Do you like the story? What is your favorite part? Why?
4) Is there anyone you have hoped would not have to go away?
5) In this story a word to describe how Amanda felt when Betty Bug flew away is peace. Peace is also in Scripture:

I have told you these things, so that in me [Jesus] you may have peace. In this world you will have trouble. But take heart! I have overcome the world.
John 16:33

6) Can you think of anything else you want to talk about or ask?

(Check out www.supposewithrose.com for free downloadable coloring pages or activities.)

Epilog
Embracing Emotions

Dear Reader,

Truth be told, the memories of the days, weeks, and months immediately following Kayla's passing are hazy and some days feel like they still are. I was by no means fully present. I felt hollow—like the inside of me is watching the outside of me go through motions. There exists some barrier to allow outside me, the part everyone can see, to embrace inside me, the part I share with select few. It's not necessarily for self-preservation, but from more of a fear of wounding others. I had myself deceived into thinking I was responsible for everyone else's emotions as well as my own and I felt I had failed.

In order to embrace my emotions, I first must choose to face them and this deception that I am responsible for everyone else. I must do this rather than running and hiding or denying the emotions exist and rather than allowing my efforts to center solely on benefitting others. As though a mirror divides the inside from the outside, I must continue to let "inside me" look "outside me" in the eyes and call her out for the shell she tends to revert into. At the same time, "outside me" needs to take the time and make the effort to accept "inside me," wrap her in a hug, and chose to keep holding onto her. Even if she resists.

Scripture:

Though one may be overpowered, two can defend themselves. A cord of three strands is not quickly broken.

Ecclesiastes 4:12

God Is Always Chasing After You

I press onward toward the goal to win the prize for which God has called me heavenward in Christ Jesus.

Philippians 3:14

Precious in the sight of the Lord is the death of his faithful servants.

Psalm 116:15

LOVE Affirmed:

We are finite. God is infinite. Let's not confuse the two. Jesus, the Word, became flesh. He has gone before us and desires we walk in His image as His children. He calls us onward.

Some things I have found helpful so far, no matter where I have been in this journey:

1)   Stay connected.

I needed, and still need, people I could share with, who will turn around and lay what I shared at the feet of Jesus in prayer, yet still trust me to do the same. At the same time, I need understanding. Ultimately, this need to stay connected is to my true audience, the One True God. Matthew 6 sets many examples before us for this. As I mentioned before, our relationship with God the Father is the most intimate relationship we have the privilege to experience. Our time with Him is precious, powerful, and purposed.

Like the butterfly Haley drew near Kayla's inspirational horse, I must choose to let the Holy Spirit of our Savior embrace and be alive within me. I must convince "outside me" to embrace my emotions in such a way that God's love can pour into and out from me. God calls and guides us to the place He has prepared on both sides of Glory.

2)   Fight for peace.

I literally took a peace lily from Kayla's services and placed it in a clear vase with a beta I named Peace, to remind myself to tend to my peace. Silly as it may seem, just those moments of going through the motions of feeding the fighting fish or tending the plant, reminded me I had to fight for peace.

Honor your loved one.

One example in their presence is to respect them and their wishes when possible. Leading up to her passing, Mom remembered things that did not happen. Rather than argue, we'd just join in her conversation. Also, Mom did not want a crowd of people marching through and crying over her with goodbyes in her last days.

Mom died in the presence of her children, in her own room and bed, with one of her cattle right outside her window, just 101 days after Kayla went home to Jesus. (The 101 number makes me smile as Kayla's favorite childhood book was *101 Dalmatians*—I think it was because it was the longest book she had at the time.)

One example of honoring Kayla was a combination of ideas from Haley. Our last adventure together with Kayla included visiting 50 parks in one year. We did this adventure in 2020, when the pandemic hit. Haley suggested we visit 50 parks again, but this time paint and leave rocks at each park, like Kayla had done in the hospital for the girl. So, in 2022 we set out on our adventures: 50 different parks. Sometimes we met with others, sometimes not; sometimes the visit was planned, sometimes spontaneous, but we always left at least one painted rock in Kayla's memory. This gave us a goal to work together towards. It allowed us to connect through creativity, and helped us say and honor Kayla's name out loud.

3) Listen to understand one another.

Haley mentioned that she felt lonely. Rather than just react with, "What about me? I am here," I listened to understand her perspective. After sharing her conversation and feelings with Dustin, praying, and coming to an agreement, we decided to let her have a dog. Tiger joined our family, and the addition of that canine companion was just what she needed. She has since gained another fur baby, Panda.

4)   Accept help.

While we were in the hospital, many individuals and organizations helped us. We felt the love of Christ through each of their actions and support. But accepting help was in itself a hard task. One we initially declined was the Ronald McDonald House. We figured our home was just 20 minutes from the hospital and didn't want to take a room from someone else. But the social worker and care team further encouraged us, and when Kayla had the extended ICU days, having a room at the hospital where Dustin could sleep and have a home-away-from-home minutes away was irreplaceable.

5)   Cookie cutter grief doesn't exist.

No borders to grief look identical. One of the hard aspects of the healing journey is when others fail to acknowledge this uniqueness to each person. If we remember there is no such thing as cookie-cutter grief, we can manage our expectations better—not only the expectations we hold of others but also expectations we hold of ourselves.

I write and talk to process things. Sometimes, my thoughts are like a ping-pong ball in a table tennis tournament. I take the same topic and pass it back and forth while I face things head on, resulting often in hard emotional hits. Big highs and big lows. This fact, among others, led me to seek counseling. Dustin, however, busies his hands and has an ability to check out from his thoughts. He will not broach the topic fully until it breaches itself.

These differences can prove troublesome between us at times, especially if they cause resentment. However, if we remember the grief and healing journey is as unique as our fingerprints, we can choose to love one another through and rejoice in our differences.

I am concluding this collection and sending it to the publisher April 14, 2023, just two years and one day since the initial call kicked off our healing journey with Kayla. To say everything is still fresh is an understatement. By no means am I a professional of anything or in any right. I do not possess any authority beyond my own actions. It is not my desire that these writings come off as such. Rather, I appeal to hurting hearts, that this sharing, this collection,

offers hope amid your healing journey and perhaps a smile or two
along the way. Whether you are the person facing your own mortality
today, whether you are tending to another's needs, or whether you
are mourning the loss of a loved one, I pray you can rest assured that
God treasures you just the way you are. He is ready and willing to be
with you just where you are. He is indeed chasing after you and
ready, willing, and able to wrap you in a love like none other, so that
in time, you may share smiles along the way.

Prayer:

Lord, I pray words found in 1 Thessalonians 2: 3–4 over this
book as it meets strong opposition in the form of ills and pains of this
world and our flesh. "For the appeal we make does not spring from
error or impure motives, nor are we trying to trick anyone. On the
contrary, we speak as those approved by God to be entrusted with the
gospel. We are not trying to please people but God, who tests our
hearts."

And Father, I pray the words found in Numbers 6: 24–26 over
each Reader and their loved ones, "The Lord bless you and keep you;
the Lord make his face shine on you and be gracious to you; the Lord
turn his face toward you and give you peace."

Smiles to Share - Epilogue

A Special Place

As a little child, I found a special place.
Before I knew the hurry-up mentality ran the human race.
It was on a Saturday when I found myself bored.
To keep idle hands busy, I decided to explore.

When I began my journey, I felt down and all alone.
I walked to a pond not too far away from home.
I saw a big-eyed catfish staring up at me.
I threw some fish food in the water out of curiosity.

When I first began, the water was calm and still.
Before I knew it, it was rough—many catfish wanted their fill.
Just as quick as it came, the rough water had come to pass.
It was left as it was found, the water smooth as glass.

I was lost in the wandering of my mind.
I went onward in my journey, a cattle trail my guide.
I was led by a butterfly, as it fluttered gracefully.
Then at last it landed beneath a leaning oak tree.

The tree's trunk was a tad too big to wrap my arms around.
It ran waist high, parallel to the ground.
This was the perfect place to rest weary feet.
So, I let them sway and dangle while I took a seat.

God Is Always Chasing After You

Just as I got comfortable, I felt a hard stare.
Frozen in caution, a female deer was there.
The doe did not bolt away nor did she avert her eyes.
When two spotted fawns appeared much to my surprise.

The doe began to graze, the fawns to frolic and play.
I could almost hear them laughing, as I looked on in dismay.
The silent laughter turned to birdsong, ringing through the trees;
As a pair of cardinals serenaded the gentle springtime breeze.

I felt special, as though my world was putting on a show.
I knew right then when I needed peace this is where I'd go.
It took time to see my special place was in me all the time.
When I let God's creation encircle me and make His word come
alive in my heart and mind.

Faith in something bigger; hope in what is yet to come.
A world of life encircled in the beauty of His unfailing love.
When you are faced with all life sometimes can bring.
Remember God accompanies you in every single thing.

Connecting Ideas:

1) Do you have a place that makes you feel special?
2) What is your favorite animal?
3) Do you like the story? What is your favorite part? Why?
4) Have you ever followed a trail like the person in the story?
5) This story includes the word "onward." Onward is also in Scripture:

I press onward toward the goal to win the prize for which God has called me heavenward in Christ Jesus.

Philippians 3:14

6) Can you think of anything else you want to talk about or ask?

Check out www.supposewithrose.com for free downloadable coloring pages or activities.)

Unfinished Utterings

Dear Reader,

I've shared a big part of my family's healing journey with you. Truth be told our healing, like yours, is unfinished and perhaps even untold. The next chapter for the purpose of this book it is yours to write. Use these pages as you wish. Write your worries as prayers. Doodle. Write a letter to someone that cannot read it. Pen blessings as praises. Let your imagination run wild. Whatever you do, I pray you choose to give your untold thoughts a voice. Remember, you are not alone.

God Is Always Chasing After You

God Is Always Chasing After You

God Is Always Chasing After You

www.ingramcontent.com/pod-product-compliance
Lightning Source LLC
Chambersburg PA
CBHW051533120626
46551CB00012B/1199